My Life With My Wife

A Husband's True Love Story
Adventure. Faith. Tragedy. Resilience.

By
Bill Leone

Published by RebelBooksPress.com
A division of The Jersey Tomato Press, LLC

Copyright © 2022 by Bill Leone

Published in the United States by RebelBooksPress.com

ISBN: 979-8-9868931-0-5

Editor: Diane Lilli

Front and back cover design by Diane Lilli

Manufactured in the United States First Edition

Dedicated to my lovely wife Diane,
who I love so much,
and miss even more.

Forever yours,
Mr. William

Table Of Contents

Introduction

I DON'T CONSIDER MYSELF to be a "smart guy", and I don't use a lot of big words, so you don't need to have a dictionary beside you when reading this book.

My thoughts are simple, and my writing is the same, but it's always written in truth and honesty.

During my younger days as a single young man, like most of us, I tested the waters in different areas of my growth process. That being said, things didn't always work out to be the way that I thought they would.

There were times when I was trying to be someone that I was never going to be, no matter how hard I worked at it, all because I was being told that this was the way it is. Fortunately, there were others in my life that would contradict those teachings.

I experienced the consequences of my bad decisions, but God remained faithful and saw fit to bring me through the tall grass. Needless to say, I survived to live on and make many more bad decisions!

In addition, I must tell you that if you do survive your life's choices, those past experiences are the ones that help you in your future to make it better for yourself, as well as for others.

What you pass on, good or bad, is what's called your legacy...it's the things you do or say that people will remember you for. Some of the choices that Diane and I made together may not have been godly choices at the time, and I don't condone or encourage that kind of behavior.

But the blessing from it all was that together, we made our lives right with God. Fruit was produced from our struggles, and most of all, so was the undying love that we shared for each other. This type of story doesn't always work out for the best, but in our case, it very much did so!

CHAPTER 1

Before It Was Us

Prevenient Grace
"...divine grace that is said to operate on the human will antecedent to its turning to God."

I'M SITTING IN A HOSPITAL ROOM next to my wife's bed, watching her sleep. You see, at this exact moment, we are experiencing what we would call an adventure. I get the idea of writing about the life that I have had with her thus far. But let's back up just a bit so I can fill you in on how we got to this point.

I've heard that every great story begins with the phrase, "Once upon a time...."

I believe that this is one of those great true love stories. But, of course, I may be a little biased. There's this sign I have hanging in my office that says, "Every love story is beautiful, but ours is my favorite!" (Author unknown.)

Once upon a time, about forty-plus years ago, the year was 1978ish, when a boy (me) met a girl whose name was Diane. Though we didn't grow up together by going to the same grammar schools and whatnot, Diane and I didn't meet until high school and then went to different ones.

She was a grade ahead of me (I always had a thing for older women!), but both schools were in the same city, which made us crosstown rivals. She was a Burbank Bulldog, and I was a Burroughs Indian. The two schools seemed to take turns as to who would win the current football season. To me, it didn't really matter much because I played baseball for the Indians, and we usually lost... to everybody!

Coincidentally, she played softball for the Bulldogs. It was a match made in heaven, and we didn't even know it yet. It was the beginning of a meaningful and lifelong friendship, love story, and adventure.

During this time, she was going steady with a friend of mine from Burroughs and spent much of her time at our school because of that relationship. I was going steady with a girl as well. But here is how we all met: through music.

Myself, the girl I was with, another guy, and two more girlfriends were in the choir together. Diane sang in the Bulldogs choir as well as being a member of their Barbershop Quartet. She had an amazing voice, by the way. It was very pure, with no frills, with just honest singing that left you feeling the music deep in your heart.

Anyway, they had organized an after-school guitar club that began in Junior High, which had quite a few members. This club carried on throughout High School. But later, a few of them broke off and formed a guitar and vocal group off campus, and would sing and perform at various homes of friends from Burbank to the Lone Pine/Bishop area.

The leader of the group was very gifted in figuring out all of the vocal parts for the girls to sing, and there were four. They really had a beautiful and tight sound, especially for just being high schoolers. All of them worked hard and had a lot of fun. But I wasn't a part of this special little group...yet.

One day our choir had just finished rehearsing for some show or concert performance that was coming up. That group had some time after the rehearsal and decided to rehearse a little bit themselves.

Diane wasn't there at the time because school was still in session. They began to sing, and the leader played the guitar and sang as well.

The piano, a beautiful nine-foot concert grand, hadn't been put away yet, and was still on the stage.

While they were all doing their thing, I decided to do mine!

I worked my way over to the piano, ever so stealth-like, sat down, and began to play along with them. Now I must say, I do play pretty decently. But, when you have a nine-foot concert grand at your fingertips, chopsticks would sound great!

In any case, they heard what I was doing and started to smile, so I just kept playing, and they kept singing. Thank the LORD, they were rehearsing a song that I knew! We all enjoyed our time together, and eventually, the leader asked me if I would like to join them.

My then-girlfriend was already in the group, so it didn't take me long to give them a very excited yes! After that day, we all would hang out together, which meant that we all got to know each other really well. We would become so close to each other that we were like family. Everyone else had at least one brother or sister or both, and some had multiple siblings.

I was an only child, and this bond that we all had with one another was very special to me. I had gained brothers and sisters that I didn't realize I wanted or needed, and it was a magical feeling.

One of the group's main activities was to travel to a place called Lone Pine, in California. The assistant principal at the time was also the overseer and a good friend of the group. We would pack up the vehicles and head out of Burbank, hitting the road to fame and fortune! Or at least a little bit of fame.

Our chaperone's mother and father had a place in Lone Pine. The parents obviously were an older, more mature couple with a lot of energy and a lively spring to their steps. They were awesome people to open their homes to us, and we loved being around them.

The property spread out across land that was not yet developed, so you felt like you were in the middle of nowhere. The terrain was not very smooth, but it was still manageable to explore on foot. There were rocks, and even huge boulders to climb and jump on.

The landscape included various types of desert trees and bushes, as well as some long grass that would turn a golden color in the summer. The sunsets were amazing, and so were the sunrises. There was even an old broken down shed and a barn that was really cool to hang out in. For water, there was a below-ground well that had a small shed-type-looking cover over it. One time, we looked inside and saw a dead rat! It was really gross to think that was in there, our drinking water. Fortunately, they had an up-to-date water filtration system which kept us safe.

The house had a half-wrap-around wooden porch that we all would sunbathe on during the day when we weren't out exploring.

When it was time for bed, all of us would spread out our sleeping bags, blankets, and pillows on the floor in this huge living room. It had tall windows that went from floor to ceiling and lined the room almost completely. On clear nights, a full moon would light up the outside and inside. It was very peaceful and beautiful, and that's where we stayed.

Now, this was all new to my single-parent mom, but she trusted me and seemed to be at ease with this special group of kids…or should I say, young adults. Also, the fact that there was an adult from the school chaperoning us helped make her decision for me to go there a little easier to make.

I'll never forget this one trip we took. We all piled in the back end of one of the group's boyfriend's big red 4x4 pickup truck that had a shell on it. And yes, it was ok to do that back then! Anyway, once we got to Lone Pine, we would take it out four-wheeling during the day, trying to make it up certain hills, kicking up dirt everywhere, and laughing and enjoying life the best way we knew how.

But when nighttime hit, well, that was a different story. Diane and her best friend at the time had nicknames for each other. Her friend's nickname was Lady, and Diane's nickname was Sunny...shortened from Sunshine. Now there's a reason I'm telling you this story because I'm about to confess to a crime.

It was one of the all-time great robbery events of the Twentieth Century! Here's what went down. Now keep in mind Diane's nickname is Sunshine.

One night we all had gotten a hold of some beer, and of course, we were feeling very brave for some reason. It must have been about one or two in the morning (if not later). While cruising down one of the many dirt roads that were available and in total darkness, I had no idea how we saw it. Still, there was this old wooden sign about a little over a foot and a half in length and about nine inches high hanging across this old swinging wooden gate that blocked a road that led to someone's ranch that had the name "Sonshine" on it!

The driver of the big red 4x4 slammed on the breaks, and he and a couple of other friends that had come along on that trip jumped out and cut the wire that held the sign to the fence! In a cloud of dust we drove off into the night without a hitch. We were all so excited about our find and steeling that sign for Diane, which by the way, she didn't ask for us to do that. I still have that sign today, and it hangs in our kitchen as a reminder of the best of times we all had together...Sonshine.

Oh, and one more little tidbit of info that I never really noticed back then was the way the ranch had spelled the word Sonshine.

You see, S...U...N is that big bright ball of fire in the sky. S...O...N refers to what you would call your offspring, or in this case, God's Son...Jesus. Also referring to the phrase, "May God's Son shine His holy light upon you."

God's prevenient grace was shining on all of us that night, and He continued to intercede with mine and Diane's future together.

A little time passed, and we found ourselves planning another trip to the Lone Pine area. But this time, we had an invitation to sing and play at home in Bishop, California, which was just a bit further away. It was beautiful up there, and the snow was on the ground.

This night's performance turned out to be a very special one because we had an extraordinary guest show up. Her name is Jill Kinmont. Some of you may remember her. She was a very talented skier that had a terrible life-threatening accident at a competition that was getting her ready for the upcoming Winter Olympics. She was only eighteen years old when her life changed forever. But that night in Bishop, she was there to hear us sing. It was quite an honor and one of the highlights of our careers as musicians.

After our house concert had concluded, we got to hang out and spend some time with Jill and all of the other guests that were there for an evening of music and just plain old enjoying each other's company. While all along, our relationships kept getting stronger together, this also meant that we all were facing different challenges and struggles in our lives. But the only difference was that we knew we were never alone, because we always had each other and had each other's backs, no matter what. And I genuinely mean, no matter what. Oh yea, by the way, this group had a name. We were called "Love & Laughter." Cute right? It later morphed into "Light Touch," but we can discuss that later.

We continued on in our lives together and as individuals. It came time for us all to graduate high school, and as luck would have it, I was fortunate enough to go to two proms!

Remember, I was a grade behind everyone, and my girlfriend at the time was one year ahead of me...I went to hers in 1979, and she went to mine in 1980.

When it was time to go to her prom (same school), our group was altogether on that eve.

Our turn came for photos. We took our couples' photos, but then we all took one of the group...Love & Laughter. As so many times before, our time together was not without some sort of unique twist. In one of Diane's softball games against another school just before the prom, one of the players on the other team was aiming to take Diane out at second base...she did. Diane still made the play but ended up in a full leg cast, hip to ankle, and then showed up in it at the prom! There was no way she was going to miss her big night out.

It was excruciating when it happened and very painful during recovery. We all danced together and still had a great time, though. At the end of the evening, we all went our separate ways until we connected again the next day to tell stories and relive the night.

If I may, let's have a "squirrel!" moment. I titled this book "My Life With My Wife," and if you haven't figured it out by now, that doesn't mean I'm only sharing our life as a married couple...No! There was a lot of life together before we were married, which makes all of this so special... at least to me.

After my friends' graduation, we would continue to play music together, travel together, and eventually, it would be time for my Senior prom.

My long-time girlfriend had a twin sister, and she and my best friend began dating. We all went to our prom together in a limo. But it wasn't just any limo. The girls had an uncle or some kind of family connection who had a limo service.

The limo was an older, all-white, classic Cadillac (I think late 60's) that had the company name of the service down the side of it in big black letters.

When we pulled up to our prom venue, with everyone noticing our cool ride, Uncle so and so got out and opened our doors. We got out, and the girls proceeded to give him a great big hug and a kiss and thanked him. You couldn't make this stuff up! Best of all, the limo was free! It was a great evening, and we all had a fun time.

After high school, time marched on, and our lives began to change once again. At one point, there was a falling out between the group and our longtime leader over, shall we say, artistic differences. Not too sure of the timeline for that event, but it happened, and that changed the dynamic of the group both musically and socially.

In between our trips and what became known as "The Great Desert Sign Heist," we decided to put on a concert. We didn't have any kind of group bank account, so any supplies that were needed came out of our pockets and by way of loving and caring family and friends.

With that in mind, one of the biggest things we needed to do to be able to have a concert was that we needed a venue...a place to perform. Some really good and supportive family and friends of ours offered their backyards, and we took them up on it. These folks are amazing people, and we don't know what we would have done without them. We invited friends and family and even sold a few tickets...what fun! Some more time passed, and we decided we wanted to do another one. So Diane's brother-in-law and older sister offered up their backyard to us. Well, we all jumped at the idea!

The concert was scheduled to take place in September 1981(I found a VHS copy the other day of that concert—it was awesome to see it again). But this time it wasn't just us at the concert...there were guest musicians! We had a horn section and another guitarist! Oh! And let's not forget that we had a sound guy as well! This was big time!

That's right! A full-on horn section—it was amazing!

We all worked really hard and rehearsed all the time. Again, the usual crowds that came were friends and family, but that made the night special—it was comfortable and safe. After much debate, our group name was changed to "Light Touch"...catchy, right?

Remember, Diane and I were not together yet. We were still perfect friends and had significant others at this time. As I said before, lives began to change. One of the couples in the group got married, and we all struggled to keep it all together. Soon, we all ended up taking a break from the group for a while. It was kind of a sad time for me because I needed to see them more than I thought I did and more than they knew.

After some more time, Diane and her high school sweetheart eventually got married—as it was the plan to do so for a long time. I was still with my sweetheart, and we not only attended that wedding, but I played the organ for all of the appropriate songs that people at weddings usually would play.

There's even a picture taken at the wedding rehearsal of her dad walking her down the aisle that shows me in the background, high up in the balcony hanging over the railing (that's where the organ was).

Can you say, "Creeper?" I have that photo still, and I laugh every time I see it. Finally, a third couple got married, where my girlfriend was a bridesmaid, and I played the organ again.

As I've said before, our events don't seem to be without some sort of extraordinary, unplanned happening. Well, it was one of the hottest days that year, and my girlfriend, standing up there in front of the whole church full of family and friends...fainted! I was watching the entire thing from the back of the church, and there wasn't a thing I could do about it. It was like watching a tree fall after it had been cut down... falling almost in slow motion. There seemed to be plenty of time to get out of its way.

She wasn't hurt because her friends that were up there with her had caught her. It was definitely not one of her best days. Still, the wedding continued, and we all had a blessed time together in celebration of the newly married couple.

At this point, I had been with her for 4 years. I was still struggling to figure out what I would do with my life as in what I wanted to be when I grew up. At the same time, she went to college and received her degree, and began working for Hollywood studios in accounting. Looking back, I should have been more proud of her than I was...she was and is, to this day, a really good-hearted person and dear friend.

Something happened along the way with our relationship, and we ended up parting ways.

It broke my heart when that happened, and I'm still not really sure why it happened. I was obviously very clueless about the reason at the time. I sometimes thought about that turn of events to this day, wondering how life would have turned out if we had stayed together, what our kids would be like, where we would be living, etc...

Oh well, that will surely remain as one of life's great mysteries... at least to me.

I may not know or understand why that breakup happened. Still, I do understand now that it had to happen for God to work His wonderful plan for the ultimate adventure that was in store for Diane and me...one that we had no idea was coming!

As time continued moving forward, the music that we all loved and made as a group just wasn't enough to keep us all together. And soon, as many people and friends do, we began to drift apart. Although we never lost the bond we all had, our priorities just seemed to change...as they should have.

Light Touch members were now married, and it was time to start concentrating on those relationships and the desire to start their families. Homes need to be bought, careers need to begin, and baby's needed to be...well, you know.

CHAPTER 2

Uncharted Waters

Psalm 119:176 "...I have strayed like a lost sheep..."

BACK IN THE 1980S, video stores were all the rage, and there was one on every corner. I landed a job on one of those corners with an independent company called "Discount Video." We not only rented videotapes, both VHS and the ever popular BETA but VCRs (Video Cassette Recorder) as well. I thought it was the best thing since sliced bread, and the employees got to take home any movies they wanted to watch for free! I was living large, alright!

But as fate would have it, soon, the little mom & pop stores were forced to close because of the bigger video store chains that also came to be on every street corner. However, I was able to break out of that industry and decided to try my hand at Jr. College, specifically in film editing.

You see, I had an uncle that was the film editor for the TV show "Get Smart" back in the 60's, and he did very well.

It was his suggestion to check out that field, and it sounded like fun. Unfortunately, I didn't make it past the first semester. I'm not sure if it was the teacher or me. All I knew was that it wasn't something that blew my dress up...music was always my main interest anyway. With that in mind, I wound up working in the Sherman Oaks Galleria for Baldwin Piano & Organ selling, and you guessed it, pianos and organs! After that, I connected with a few different organ manufacturers and became a Product Specialist/Concert Artist.

I traveled the country to train sales staff and their customers on the instruments.

In the evenings, I would then put on a little in-store concert to top off the day. I was single with no real responsibilities, and I really enjoyed it at the time.

Meanwhile, back at the ranch, Diane had landed a job with the Burbank Police Department. If I remember correctly, she was the executive secretary for two of the captains.

Her father was a detective there and later retired with that rank. It was during this time that she and her husband started having kids. The funny thing about that I was still close friends with them, and I was around for all of the births of their kids. In time, I became...Uncle Bill. Remember this for later, because later it will get a little comical with my titles.

Some years had passed, and the Piano and Organ biz began to die off, and artists weren't much needed any longer. This meant that I needed to find something else to do. So, I ended up in the customer service field as well as working in shipping and receiving.

At this point, you can understand why I was a lost sheep. Not only was my so-called career non-existent, and I had no girlfriend, but my faith was not really there either. I did believe in God somewhat but didn't know about Him and didn't make much of an effort to do so.

It was about this time when Diane, myself, and one of the other members of "Light Touch" started talking again about how much we missed just getting together and making music. We then decided we would make it happen and began rehearsing and learning new songs—getting together once a week or so at my house (still in the 80's).

We eventually had enough material together where we could actually play at parties and wedding ceremonies. As we had changed our group name just before our last concert to "Light Touch," the three of us decided to keep the name for our little trio.

At one point, we even had some business cards made. This was before you could do that on a computer!

We sounded pretty good, if I do say so myself. And once again, there was that something special that happened to make our time together stand out. I'll never forget one time when we were asked to provide the music for a backyard wedding ceremony. They had a pool, and we were stationed at one end of it.

During one of the songs, the girls looked up and saw this lone Kamikaze pigeon flying right at them.

By the way, Diane and our friend both looked beautiful in these really unique dresses. So here's what happened. In the middle of the song, as though it was a precision air strike, this pigeon released an A-Bomb dropping as if it were a flock of pigeons. It hit the front of Diane's gorgeous green dress from knees to chest. Nothing could have been a more strategic or calculated attack. But I must say, I was very proud of them both for how they handled the Blitzkrieg. They were true professionals and kept right on singing through all of the laughter and gasps in horror. Life blazed on!

Diane has a big family, and every holiday there would be a family party. These are amazingly loving and fun people to be around. Fortunately, for me, I was always invited, and I always showed up. The times we all spent together were priceless and meant everything to me. I really can't say enough good stuff about all of them, including her parents and how they accepted me as part of the family. At least that's how they all made me feel.

Throughout this time, I had been in and out of different relationships and was almost married a couple of times. Can't tell you how thankful I was that those marriages never happened! Even though my faithfulness was weak, God's faithfulness remained strong and steadfast as He continued to watch over me.

During this time, one thing that was very special for me was that I could talk to Diane about those relationships as if she was my sister. Diane knew about all of the relationships I've ever had over the years.

She knew about the ones that broke my heart and the ones whose hearts I broke. She counseled me in tough times, and I would try to do the same for her. I knew I could go to her with anything on my mind—I trusted her with my heart and with all of my deepest, darkest secrets.

She told me the truth in a way that was so comforting, yet to the point. As sweet a singing voice that she had, her speaking voice was the same...I could listen to her for hours.

Now, most of my friends were girls. I spent a lot of time watching and learning how they work—mostly gleaning insights from the girls that were in "Love & Laughter (and "Light Touch"), Diane included. But believe me, there was a great bit of trial and error involved on my part. So please don't think I'm claiming to be some sort of expert on the workings of females. However, I can say this: I was a quick learner!

We still weren't together yet, but we were together in some unexplainable way. I must confess that from the moment I first met her, I felt this amazing and different connection with her that I have never felt before with anyone else...ever! I'm not sure I can explain it very well...maybe I can call it a soul connection. At the risk of sounding corny or like a cliche, she made my whole body just tingle with joy to be around her.

It's almost like the excitement a puppy feels when they see you walk through the door at the end of a long day at work. It was a connection that wasn't necessarily a "head over heels" in love type of feeling— until then.

Remember, leading up to this moment in time, our little trio was still getting together once a week at my house for a rehearsal.

Now it's been said that your body changes every seven years. Just how true that really is, I'm not sure, and what areas exactly change within you, and to what extent, I don't know. But what I do know is that feelings began to change between Diane and me. Our eyes began to see one another in a different light. Our hearts began being pulled in a direction that they shouldn't have been allowed to be pulled in. Feelings began to change towards each other. We must have been at the beginning of one of those seven-year cycles.

It was both exciting and terrifying all at the same time. Needless to say, the winds of change began blowing very hard and seemingly out of control.

As you may have already guessed, things were not only deeply connected on an emotional level but soon became physical as well. Now please don't be upset with me for not going into all of the dramatic details of the affair because that is not the purpose of these writings. Everything that I'm sharing with you today is simply a background on how I came to fall, and remain in love with my girl. If you want something to chew on for a bit, picture the movie "Bridges of Madison County," but without the farm animals and with a much different ending! Also, and most importantly, let me make it clear, I wasn't a pastor yet!

Flashing back to a Lone Pine trip, I remember one evening at the house where we stayed. I had wandered off into the darkness not too far from the house. Although it really wasn't that dark because the stars, and full moon, were very bright and lit up the ground like daytime—it was beautiful.

I turned around to see this silhouette coming toward me. At first, I was a bit scared, but then I could make out what and who it was—it was Diane. We chatted a bit, and then she asked me a most interesting and unexpected question.

She asked me if I thought that she and I should be together, as in boyfriend and girlfriend. I completely froze and had a deer in the headlights kind of moment and gave her an answer that I would deeply regret and kick myself for years and years to come. I actually turned her down while my insides were screaming yes! Yes! Say yes, you idiot! But in my now infinite wisdom, I can look back and see that I really wasn't ready for her yet. You know, the whole girls mature faster than boys thing? (*wink*).

Our bond and our love grew stronger and stronger every day. If there was any chance to just see each other if only for a few moments, we took it; I just needed to be around her, and her me.

At one point, we were beginning to feel like we should end this type of relationship, and our hearts were both being torn apart by the possibility of having to make such a decision. One evening, we were able to sneak away for dinner at a restaurant far away from town. She had to use the ladies' room, and while she was away, I was thinking to myself, how can you continue to do this to her and her family? I was working up the courage to put an end to this chapter of our lives because I fully knew that she would have to endure much more than I would if we were to continue on this path.

When she came back to the table, I started off by saying to her, "I'm going to make it easy for you." Right then and there, she stopped me dead in my tracks so I couldn't finish my thought, and she said, "I knew you were going to say that". Her next statement went like this, "I don't want you to make it easy for me." It was at that point, I knew that we were both, as they say, in it to win it! In the months to come, our lives began changing from day to day. As many good days as there were, there were as many, if not more bad days. The mix of different emotions was almost unbearable at times.

But through all of the stress and heartache we faced, our love for each other remained strong and continued to grow. During this turbulent time, I would try to do as many things as possible to encourage and remind her that I was still there, that I wanted to be with her always, and that she was worth the struggle. Also, I needed her to know that she was always in my heart and on my mind.

One of those things that I oh so cleverly did happened early one day when I had made these three signs. I attached them to three light posts on the side of a particular road she would drive every morning while she was on her way to drop kids off at school and then on to begin her work day. Her favorite animal was piggies —she was crazy about them! On each of the signs, I drew a picture of a piggy. But, there was also a number written on each of the signs...1, 4, 3. It was her code that told me that she loved me. 1=I, 4=Love, and 3=You. I made them kind of big and was glad that I didn't get caught doing this by the police or anyone else, for that matter!

There were other things that I had strategically placed in her path to see that would remind her of me.

Certain songs that we latched onto as being our song per se helped us to stay somewhat sane and connected to each other when we weren't able to be together.

Examples are: "More Than Words Can Say" by Alias; "Anything For You" by Gloria Estefan; "Go Away" by Steve Perry, and multiple songs by the group Surface such as "The First Time";

"Never Gonna Let You Down"; and a few others. But I saved the best for last—"Get Here" by Oleda Adams.

I remember thinking to myself that if we can make it through this, we can make it through anything—and we did—except for this one thing. I'll share this one thing with you all much later. Life went on as normal (for the most part).

The various holiday family gatherings still happened, kids' birthday parties were still being celebrated, and swim parties and BBQs took place. All the while, no one had a clue of the love and the relationship that was building between us. Let me once again say, that I'm not trying to glorify how we came to be together in this way, nor am I making any kind of an attempt to justify our actions.

People were hurt, and relationships were damaged, to say the least. But if these losses had to be endured for us to be together, then I was willing to endure those hardships. For me, the losses were worth the gains.

Things had progressed in a bad direction between Diane and her husband, and efforts were made to try and repair their relationship through various means of personal therapy and couple/marriage counseling.

I was in agreement with her for doing this because we both wanted to make sure that this relationship was more than an escape route for her. It felt like the right thing to do in the midst of so many wrong things that had been happening. To quote my kids with a line they would use often, "I'm not gonna lie," I was hoping that the therapy and counseling didn't work—I know, you all don't have to tell me... I'm a jerk! But honestly, it was the way I was feeling. I didn't want to lose her.

After many failed attempts at seeking guidance, both spiritually and secular, it came to the realization for Diane that the marriage was over. I was proud of her for trying, but her husband's effort wasn't mutual. I'm not gonna lie. For me, I was relieved. At this point, things began coming to a head, and quickly! Now up to this point, Diane and I had started talking about when it would be a good time to let everyone know about her and me.

Actually, there was no such thing as a good time to have such a conversation.

This girl was one of the bravest people I ever knew. She started at the top and worked her way down—her husband first. She and I knew this time was coming. I wasn't sure if I would end up shot dead in an alley and then dumped in a ditch or be forever brokenhearted and not be with my one and only true love of my life.

Although the more I think about it, looking back, I feel that being brokenhearted and not being with her would have been the worst of the two.

Leading up to this chain of events, I was very alone. There wasn't anyone I could have talked to about this or shared my heartache with. So as God would have it, He used this time to draw me closer to Him (prevenient grace). Let me explain, if I may, and share a brief testimony.

There was this park that I went to as a kid, and I have many good memories of growing up there. It soon became my church. I had always believed in God, but as I said earlier, I never pursued Him or any relationship with Him. I've learned over the years that God seems to be able to do His best work with us when we come to Him broken, with nothing to lose in this state of being. This was me 100%!

Anyway, back to the park...my church. I would go there late at night and just sit there, looking up into the sky, but I needed something to focus on. I soon found the moon or a constellation known as Orion to focus on as I looked upward to the Heavens. More specifically, the three stars lined up to make Orion's Belt. I knew one constellation from being in the Boy Scouts as a kid. Still, to this day, I think I remain the undisputed record holder for being the longest-running Tenderfoot in scouting history (that's the first rank you have as a newbie).

I would sit at one end of a picnic table, look up and just say whatever came out of my mouth.

Tears were flowing as if the dam had just broke! But something wonderful happened one night.

I came to the point of release and turned over all of my anxiety and concerns, surrendered my will to the LORD, and accepted Him into my life. There was no band of angels singing, and the clouds didn't burst open while an earthquake shook the ground.

Everyone's experience is different when that event takes place in their lives. It means something different to folks, and people react to it differently; it's a completely unique and individual time for all who become a believer. Although something did happen.

I felt the most incredible sense of deep peace come over me. And at the risk of sounding like a cliche again, it was like a ton of bricks were lifted off my chest... literally!

There was a warm feeling moving throughout my body, and it felt good. Even though I still didn't really understand what had just happened and where I was to go from there, I thought that I was on the right path. Diane was always a bit further along with her walk than I was—more on that later.

FYI, her husband had no faith, and didn't even seem to want to entertain the idea or possibility that there is something, or to be more direct, someone out there that created the heavens and the earth and all things in them who loves you. That hurt Diane deeply. Maybe there really is something to that equally yoked thing.

2 Corinthians 6:14 *"Do not be yoked together with unbelievers. For what do righteousness and wickedness have in common? Or what fellowship can light have with darkness?"*

From then on, my life began to change— for the better.

We had entered the 1990s, and as the days passed, her husband eventually moved out, and the divorce came into effect. I soon moved in after that.

It was another life-changing event for me, with totally different responsibilities, not only to my girl but to the kids, as well as for her towards me. It goes without saying that I was petrified but also very excited for the new adventure to begin, mainly because we were on it together! FINALLY!

CHAPTER 3

The "M" Word

1 Corinthians 13:13 "And now these three remain faith, hope, and love. But the greatest of these is love."

BY NOW, IT WAS SAFE to begin letting people know and see that we were together as a couple, and in steps my dad. He was quite a character and had a tough upbringing, which seemed to stay with him into his later years. He tried to bring me up and teach me the ways of life as best he could. All in all, I loved my dad and still miss him to this day.

One of his favorite things to do to me was this: anytime I would start seeing any girl for any length of time, he would start in on me with this question: "When are you gonna make me a grandpa?" Well, I figured this time that I would show him and give him three right out the gate! Take that, Dad!

Diane and I had been living together now for about a year or so, and I was still trying to settle into a very new family dynamic. This was my first time ever living with any of my love interests. Up until this time, my mom and I had shared a house. It was the perfect setup. The house was long and had a pool and a jacuzzi in the backyard. My mom had the whole front of the house to herself, and I had the back half, with the kitchen separating the two areas.

At times, neither of us could tell if the other one was home or not. It was perfect. We split the bills and whatnots and got along really well. Since I'm an only child, I was able to keep an eye on her better and help her with whatever needs that she may have had.

Oh! And one more squirrel moment. I have to talk about the pool. It was amazing; at least, we all thought so.

It was a fairly good-sized pool, straight in its form, meaning that there were no funny curves or anything like that. But, it had a swim-up bar with four cement bar stools in the water! On the outside of the pool, there was a full wet bar that you could walk down a few steps and be at eye level with whoever was sitting on the bar stools in the water. There was a gazebo-type covering over the top of the bar. It was truly a party pool, and we all had a blast in the summers.

By the way, Diane and the kids, along with our other mutual friends, used to come over before any shenanigans had begun between us and then continued after they had as well.

There were many growing pains to address after I had moved in, but I'll get into that part more when we get to the kids' chapter. At this point, it was getting to be time for me to pop the big question. I wanted to be married to her more than anything.

I even had the ring all ready to go, and I was just trying to figure out in my small mind how and when. Well, that was pretty much decided for me when one of her sisters (who, by the way, have all been very supportive, including her brother, about our being together) cornered me one day and asked me when I was going to make Diane an honest woman. I thought to myself that I had better take advantage of this opportunity.

I told her sister that I needed someone to watch the kids for a while, and she, of course, volunteered. But before I took my girl on this very special evening, I wanted to be respectful and do right by her folks. So one night prior to the big date, I had made arrangements to go see them, and old-fashioned me, I was going to ask her father for Diane's hand in marriage. I think he replied with something like, "Hell! You can have both of them!"

I was very happy to hear this because I don't know what I would have done if he had said no. Can you say, "AWKWARD?"

Prior to all of the above, I had taken Diane to my park, and I shared with her all I was going through there late at night. I had set my watch to go off at 10:10 pm.

That was the signal telling us that it was time for her to go home when we had our rendezvous.

This time is important to remember for later. Anyway, I thought it would be really special to ask her to marry me there. The big date night had finally come, and Diane's sister had just shown up at the house (I believe it was a Thursday evening) to babysit for us (as pre-planned) so we could go out.

Where we went is a fog to me now because I was more focused on the real reason as to why we were out to begin with! And why on earth did I pick a Thursday? Oh well...

After we were done with our dinner, we eventually arrived at my/our park. We were sitting on the picnic bench, all snuggled up together as we had done so many times before, and all of a sudden, my watch alarm went off. And at what time do you think it was? You guessed it! 10:10 pm! This is how I proposed to her. While the alarm was going off, I asked her, "Do you know what time it is?". And she answered, "What time is it?" I replied, "It's time to ask you to marry me."

I don't think she thought that I was serious because she then responded with, "Don't tease me." At this point, her demeanor changed, and she soon realized that I was serious. I then proceeded to drop down on the traditional knee (cause, as you all know, I'm old-fashioned like that) and officially asked her to marry me, ring and all.

I had designed the ring and had it made special for her. It looked so good on her and didn't belong on any other hand but hers. Oh, and in case you were wondering, she said, "Yes!" through heartfelt tears of joy. I was the happiest man on earth! Thus began another such welcomed life-changing moment.

A little FYI, and to quote Joan Rivers, "Can we talk?" I must confess something. I had thought, no, dreamed about this moment for a very long time. Diane meant the world to me, and now I get to show her for the rest of our lives together. I have been blessed! Another quick sidebar, if I may. We also have two wedding anniversaries to celebrate...let me explain.

We wanted to get married in the church that we were attending. I think it was more for me than for her because I had never had that experience. I wanted to know what it was like, especially with her, even though she had already 'been there and done that.'

We went to our pastor at the time and filled him in on our great news. And then, we were met with one small obstacle: we were living together already. This posed a problem for the church. They wanted me to move out until the wedding day, but Diane and I thought that it may add more trauma to the children. They had already seen one man leave their home, and we didn't want them to see another one do the same. Not to mention, I was more settled in and contributing to all of the household functions by now.

The pastor understood our situation and came up with another option which was to get married now and then have a church wedding at a later date. So guess what happened? We got married ASAP!

Can you guess where we held the ASAP wedding ceremony? That's right: at my first church, the park. It was a small gathering, just enough to make it legal, but it was very real all the same. There was the pastor, myself and Diane, my mom, and Diane's mom and dad for witnesses, and I think even a few birds and squirrels showed up to provide the music!

Let me just share one thing with you. Now, I have been to this park a million times before.

But today, on this most important and happy day, while on the way to the park, my mom was riding with Diane and me, and Diane's folks were following us as well as the pastor in his car. Well, as history has proven time and time again, something went a little haywire. I forgot to turn down the street that the park was on! Yep! How many times had I been there before?

I flew right past it! If no one had said anything, I don't know where I would've ended up!

As you can imagine, I never lived that one down, especially from Diane's father. After we all arrived, the ceremony began, and she looked amazing as always. Of course, I was nervous... and I can't understand why? (*wink*)!

She didn't wear a wedding dress, and I didn't wear a tux, but we were dressed in nice clothes— nicer than a casual dress. We said our vows and I do's, kissed, and just like that, we were married. To hear her tell her vows, knowing that she was willing to commit her life to me, just persuaded me even more to have the same dedication and loving devotion towards her. She was a woman of her word, and I knew that she didn't take something as important as this lightly. It was a very good day.

Soon after the ASAP wedding, we began planning for the CHURCH wedding, which we set a date for January 1, that's right, on New Year's Day. If you ever want to know who your friends really are, plan a life-changing event on one of the biggest football days of the year, and see just who shows up for you.

That day was incredible in itself. The church had this great, big, beautiful stained glass window located right above the altar, but it was being blocked by a Christmas tree. We asked if they could please move it because we loved seeing it when the sun shone through it. The staff made it happen for us. They were awesome!

All of our friends and family showed up (mostly), and it was a beautiful ceremony, just like the ASAP wedding. My best friend was my best man as I was his for his wedding. After he seated the moms, he then brought down a single rose and placed it in an empty chair for my grandma, who had passed away—it was really nice to have her represented.

We said our vows, lit candles, then said our I do's, kissed, and went off to the reception. We didn't have a limo, so we used my lifted Jeep! It was fun trying to stuff Diane in the back seat with her big wedding dress train, but we both fit, and my best man was our chauffeur. I can't even begin to share with you all of the emotions that I was feeling during this whirlwind of events. C'mon! Not one, but two weddings? And kids already?

There is one emotion that I have no trouble sharing with you all, and that is the feeling of great joy and of complete and total happiness because *"I have found the one whom my soul loves"* (Song of Solomon 3:4). So there you have the story behind our two wedding anniversaries.

Eventually, we found ourselves on our way to Florida for the honeymoon. Our kids and pets were all taken care of while we were gone by our awesome family and friends. We didn't have to worry about who they were with while we spent the night in a nice hotel as well as for the duration of our honeymoon.

After we checked in, we made our way over to the elevator, stepped inside, and all of these giant people got in as well. I was a bit worried at the time because elevators do have weight limits. We came to find out a little later that they were the San Diego Chargers!

FYI, just before our arrival in Florida, while at the reception, my best friend's wife had taken it upon herself to not let Diane's champagne glass never become empty. She was very good at completing the task! Also, you should know that Diane really didn't do well with consuming a lot of champagne. This made our honeymoon night a little bit nauseating if you catch my drift.

For me, it was just another wonderful memory that I can look back on during our life together.

We woke up the next morning, packed up, checked out, hangovers and all, and headed to our destination: the ship! The trip was amazing. We went snorkeling (the water was beautiful and so clear); I shot skeet off of the side of the ship; we explored Cozumel and ate...and ate...and then ate some more.

There was this one thing that kind of freaked me out a bit, only because I hadn't ever been on a cruise ship before. That was the site of barf bags taped to the walls —everywhere!

Anyway, while on the ship, one night we were invited to dine with the captain because we were newlyweds. That was fun, and the waiters were very cool. We also met and hung out a bit with an older, also newlywed couple. They had bought us a bottle of wine one night to take back to our room. We had dinner with them on another night. It was a little late, and the restaurant was starting to close down.

Well, as luck would have it, there happened to be a very nice piano in there. I asked the Maître d' if he minded if I played a song for my wife. I assured him that I knew what I was doing and that I wasn't drunk. He chuckled and said it would be okay. It was just the four of us in there besides the staff, and I began to play one of our songs. It was Kathy Mattea's "Where've You Been." I'll never forget the look on my new wife's sweet face. It was one of pure love, and she was just beaming, watching, and listening to me play.

Softness and gentleness were also in her gaze. Those few moments melted my heart. From the movie "Somewhere In Time," picture the look that Jane Seymour had on her face when Christopher Reeve walked in on her backstage photo shoot after the play. It was that kind of look. The kind that you can feel throughout your entire body. I played that song for her that night like I have never played it before.

Our honeymoon was coming to an end, and soon we would be leaving the ship to go back home. I think it was the night before when I began feeling very sad. I couldn't figure out why until it hit me. I wasn't ready for this time to be over and didn't want to go home yet; and actually shed some tears about it.

Diane didn't know what was happening and was a bit worried until I explained to her why I was feeling like this. You see, we didn't have the traditional start-up as many married couples experience. There were already kids involved. Please don't get me wrong, I love those kids as my own, but I really wanted more time with just her. This seemed to be one of my biggest desires that I chased after throughout our entire married life. She smiled at me and calmed me down as only she could, and we came home with many beautiful pictures and some great memories.

CHAPTER 4

Kids!

Colossians 3:20 "Children, obey your parents in everything, for this pleases the Lord."

LET THE SHOW BEGIN!

There wasn't much time to relish in the afterglow of the honeymoon because, as you all know, we both came back hitting the ground running! I was actually kind of proud of us (mostly me) for being able to jump back into family life almost, seemingly, not skipping a beat.

Diane was already good at it, and I was very excited to begin the life I had always wanted with the woman that I always wanted to be with. I wish you could have seen her in action with these kids.

She was a natural at being a mom, and I learned a lot from her. She also made a great Nana and was much better at that than I am at being a Papa. I really admired her on-the-fly ability to fix and deal with things within our family unit.

Let me reiterate how much of a culture shock this whole kids and sibling thing was to me. Remember I said that I was an only child? Well, that meant that I was not used to or had any experience with siblings and how they interacted with each other. Sometimes I would look at them and just wonder to myself, why are you doing this to your brother or sister? Or, how it used to bother me every time they would get into arguments.

I never had that happen to me because I was always the king! This was a whole new world for me, but I was willing to learn it and adapt to it because I loved them, and I loved their mom.

The learning curve was great, and I was very glad that there wasn't going to be a test at the end of the day! It seemed like just when I thought I had it figured out, something new would rear its ugly head, and then I would have to start all over again! I sometimes wish that it could have all been filmed.

I'm sure it would have made for a hilarious reality show. For example, one day after I had gotten off work, which was usually around 2 - 3 o'clock in the afternoon, as always, I came home and tried to get the kids working on their chores and homework and whatnot. Well, this one day was particularly eventful.

Our middle daughter had the chore of vacuuming that day because the chore duties would rotate, and it was her turn. I happened to be on the phone with Diane (she was at work) when all of a sudden I heard this loud static pop! I told Diane that I had to go because I heard something that didn't sound right, and I would call her right back. I ran into the hallway where our daughter was, and she was standing there with the vacuum in hand, crying and screaming while the electrical socket on the wall was shorting out. The socket caused a continuous flash of electrical flame and left a large black mark on the wall!

Her hands were a little blackened, but luckily she was okay. I was a bit concerned that there may be a fire brewing within the walls of the hallway and called the Fire Department. They came with lights and sirens, and there must have been about two or three trucks that showed up. The firemen came inside and checked everything, including my daughter, and assured me there was nothing to worry about—no fire in the wall. Praise the LORD!

In the meantime, all of the neighborhood kids (including mine) were out front, climbing all over the fire trucks and having a good old time! The firemen soon departed, and while they were loading up, I decided to call Diane back. She answered her phone, and with a stressful tone to her voice, asked me what happened.

I proceeded to inform her that the fire department was just leaving and that her daughter didn't get electrocuted. Oh, and we needed a new vacuum. Not realizing how all of this must have sounded to her. I wish I could have seen the look on her face. We can all laugh about it now, but looking back, here I was being entrusted with the most precious parts of her existence, and I had to call the fire department for help! That'll scramble your eggs!

I'm sure that many of you who have multiple children know that each one has its own individuality about them. I discovered this quickly. The oldest, a boy, was very strong-willed and bullheaded. It was revealed to me much, much later in life that he used to lay down his Jax in the hallway as land mines, hoping that I would step on them in the middle of the night.

Thankfully, that never happened. When I look back at that time, I feel it was just him acting out his anger and frustration over the divorce, and I can't say I blame him. He was the oldest when it all took place, about 8 or 9.

Things eventually changed for the better, and he grew into an amazingly talented and gifted man whom I'm very, very proud of. The middle child, a girl, was always bubbly, happy, and carefree. She had a great big heart and a natural desire to care for people and animals, always a joy to be around. And finally, the youngest, another girl... she was the fireball, the athlete, the one who wanted to please everyone and could never tell a lie. She worked hard at everything she did, and the results always showed it.

There were definitely growing pains to endure throughout the years to come. Through it all, I still loved my kids, who were biologically Diane's children, that were really just an extension of her. It was worth the challenges that I faced.

Here's just a random thing that happened to us.

Diane and I decided to steal away for a bit to our favorite park. Now mind you, it's late at night, and the park is actually closed, but we weren't paying attention to the time. She had packed up a few snacks and some soft drinks, and as we were sitting there enjoying them, a police officer approached us to see what we were up to.

Almost immediately, Diane broke into tears, trying to explain to the officer that we had four children (at the time) and we just needed a break for a minute. I wish you could have seen the look on the officer's face. He had no idea what she was going to say!

He was so sweet and understanding because he could see that we weren't going to cause any problems for the neighborhood. This poor policeman then tried to calm her down and told her/us that it was okay and to take our time. She thanked him, and he said, "Enjoy your evening," and left.

The time soon came when the dreaded flu made its presence known to the household before it was called Coronavirus. Sometimes all three kids were sick, and sometimes only one at a time. But sooner or later, we all would get it as it traveled throughout the house like the plague. Now we all know what comes with flu bugs, right? Upset stomachs and potty issues, to say the least.

It's no secret that I have never been able to handle either one of those issues regarding having to clean up after such an event. In fact, I must confess that one time, we were going through one such period. A quick setup is needed here, if I may.

At different times in our life together, we would take turns as to who would work a second job for a bit. As it turned out, this was one of those times when it was Diane's turn to work the second job, and it was in the evening.

A cataclysmic happening that came to be known as "The Great Spew" occurred. I think it was our middle girl who was sick and was just about ready to blow. Well, she did! Everywhere in the house! I didn't know what to do. So the first thing I thought of was to grab a bunch of paper towels and strategically place them on top of the spewed areas, which included the walls.

That was all I could do because if I continued any further, I guarantee you that there would be an even greater mess! Yep...I left it for my loving wife to take care of when she got home after working her second job. I guess Diane never really understood the gravity of my weakness in such events, but she did now.

I know what y'all are thinking, and it's okay because I have owned up to my shortcomings in that field for a long, long time! You can only imagine what effect it had on me seeing those Barf Bags taped to the walls on the cruise ship, and

fortunately, they were empty! Soon after that incident, we came up with a plan that, for the most part, we were able to follow.

Her duties were to handle the poop and puke, and my duties were to handle the blood and guts because Diane had a weak stomach in those areas. I got to see that in action once, and it wasn't pretty.

The kids began growing, and soon my beloved Jeep was no longer suitable to carry all of us. Diane had an Aerostar minivan, but I needed something too, since we often had to split up for various activities and such.

She knew how much that Jeep meant to me because I had finally got it to the way I wanted it, and Diane had just bought a new soft top for it a little while back. It looked great! We ended up selling it, and we purchased our first Suburban. It was a beast, but it did the job for many years to come.

Looking back, it really was a small sacrifice to make for your family. I loved my girl and would've given up so much more if I needed to; I always hoped that she knew that.

At a later time, she found this little cartoon, the ones that would start off with the phrase, "Love is..." and then there would be a short little explanation of what love is. In one instance, it was a picture of the little guy pushing his Harley, with a for sale sign on it, and the caption read, "Selling your prized possession to buy her an engagement ring." Diane cut it out and wrote a note on it saying that it reminded her of when I sold the Jeep and that she loved me.

Diane would place subtle notes and things like that for me. Sometimes they would show up in my lunch box, taped to the bathroom mirror, or even hidden in my Bible. It's amazing how a gesture so small can mean so much and make you feel so good.

So you guys remember my dad with the whole "When are you going to make me a grandpa" comment, right? Well, guess what he started in on me with now? You guessed it, I bet! He would say, "When are you going to have one of your own?"

Oy! But little did he know, Diane and I were already thinking about it anyway, and we were talking about it even more.

It didn't take long to make the decision to go for it. Again, I have never experienced such an event from start to finish, and couldn't be happier than to experience this with my best girl. Knowing that she wanted to have a child with me made my heart for her grow bigger and bigger. This was a big deal, and it meant as much to me. Just when you think you can't love someone any more than you already do, something like this comes along, and you can.

Soon, Diane became pregnant with our youngest son, and he brought the kid count to four for us. I didn't want to know what sex the baby was because, like I said a while ago, I had never experienced such a thing, and wanted it to be a surprise. He was born in 1995.

At one point, just before his birth, the doctor warned us that there was a good chance that he may be born with Down Syndrome because of some findings that showed up from a test they had run on the amniotic fluid. They proceeded to talk to us about options, and mostly the option of abortion. Well, we were having none of that and made it perfectly clear of what we wanted. We had begun to prepare for the possibility of having a special needs child and were already in love with and committed to our baby no matter what. He was ours.

But God hadn't spoken just yet. The day came for our child's grand entrance into the world, and he ended up being a C-section. Lo and behold, our little miracle came out absolutely perfect! There were no issues whatsoever!

Now church, let me remind y'all of something; when doctors can't, God can! We were greatly blessed. God is good all the time, and all the time, God is good! After his birth, we moved to a bigger house and got back into Burbank, for we had been living in Sun Valley at the time.

God blessed us again (with a little help from my mom) and provided a six-bedroom, three bathroom home. Each kid was able to have their own room. Do I need to mention that they were very happy about that?

The youngest and newest addition grew up with love for athletics, but most of all, a deep love for music, and I don't mean just listening to it. He made music! This one can play multiple instruments (got that from me), sing incredibly well (got that from his mom), as well as be able to compose/arrange for himself and for others. He also has a big heart for people, and they know who to come to when they need an ear to listen.

God blessed me with an amazing woman, and she blessed me with an amazing family.

This new season of life brought us countless choir events, baseball games, soccer games, football, and basketball games, and let's not forget about the cheerleading events! I especially enjoyed the back-to-school nights. Oh what fun... NOT! You see, we had a kid in every type of school, which included: pre-school, grammar school, middle school, and high school, and of course, all of them shared the same date for back-to-school night! Diane and I had to split up where she would take two, and I would take the other two. What a night! Anyway, we survived as always, and would later meet back at home.

Even though Diane and I had to be separated for part of the evening, I knew that we would be back together soon—not being with her was the worst part of life for me. That welcomed pain only grew bigger as time went on. I say welcomed pain because it was an ache in my heart that I knew would soon go away. It gave me something to look forward to, in reuniting with her rather than not being with her at all. They say it's good to miss someone sometimes...maybe it is.

There were, of course animals. The children had a desert turtle already and so did I. This one day, our Alaskan Malamute decided to play with one of them and flipped him in the hot sun. We didn't catch it in time...back to one turtle (still have him). A few dogs, a cat to which I was allergic, lizards, hamsters, and guinea pigs, all rounded off our menagerie.

I had mentioned a while back that I had many different names that the kids would call me. At first, before marriage, it was Uncle Bill because I had been in the picture before, during, and after their births. After we were married, it morphed into Uncle Bill Bill, and soon into Uncle Daddy Bill, Daddy Bill, and then moving on to Dad. I never put pressure on the kids to call me anything other than what they felt comfortable with calling me until, one day, something happened.

I had noticed that the titles would change every so often, and I paid close attention to why. I soon discovered that when they got mad at me for whatever reason, I was called Bill.

But when everything was all hunky dory, it was dad or daddy Bill. For some reason that didn't sit right with me, and this was the only time I stressed to them what to call me. I simply said to pick one and stay with it no matter what you felt towards me. Eventually, it was DAD. However, the one Diane and I had together didn't have any other options but to call me DAD!

We came to be known as a blended family, but the reality of it for me was that they were MY kids, and I loved them. In turn, that translated to Diane as to how much I loved her without question. When you love someone, you love everything about them— including their children, and claim them as your own whether you adopt them or not. You commit wholeheartedly and love them completely.

I believe the phrase these days besides "go big or go home" is, "send it!" and I did. All of us went on to spend many fantastic vacations and outings together that have provided so many good memories for me. Not to mention all of the fun mishaps and randomness that occurred. We were blessed!

As our kids got bigger, so did the problems that we faced with them. One of the best things that Diane and I would do was to ride our bicycles together. Soon, this became a way for us to break away for a bit to discuss and solve the world's problems. This was a real and much needed thing for us to go on a ride.

We had a bike path close to our house, and we would head for it and follow it until we were satisfied with the solutions to the issue or issues at hand. Some hard decisions were made on those rides. But we felt good about those decisions and mostly the outcomes from them. We, of course, would pray over the ride and over what God may reveal to us in the form of what direction to go.

Some of the best conversations we had were on that bike path. Still, the most important thing was that we were united, together, and committed to working on our family together. Whatever challenges we faced, we did so as Husband and Wife, and as friends. You see, unlike many couples that I hear of, and see these days, they don't like each other or like being around each other very much, whether they say so or not. You can see it. I really liked my girl and always wanted to be around her. I knew in my heart that I could not have done it alone, and was so thankful to have a woman like Diane by my side through everything. I miss those times so much.

The kids continued to grow and tried to find their ways in life. As I stated before, there were many challenges and struggles that they faced alone. I say alone because things were going on that they never disclosed to us. Eventually, after it had passed, we would hear about the event or events that took place. All the while, mom and dad were continuing to pray that God watches over and protect the kids, and He did!

Let me share something with you. I'm writing about my incredible, deep love story with my wife. But that can't happen without sharing the fact that I love my children, too. For that in itself is a love story but of a different type of love. To be more clear, they are part of what has made me and continues to do so, to be the man that I am today.

I'll be forever grateful, and love them for the opportunity they have given me, earning the honor to be called Dad.

As the sands of time continued to flow, life was about to change in very dramatic and unforeseen ways. Our kids were beginning to form close relationships with others. They were the kind that would last a long time. And one of those

relationships was between our oldest daughter and a friend of hers, a girl from middle school. They were together most of the time and really seemed to connect with one another. Little did we know that new challenges and blessings were soon to come our way.

Ready or not, here they come!

CHAPTER 5

Number 5

Matthew 18:5 "And whoever welcomes one such child in my name welcomes me."

ONE OF THE MOST BEAUTIFUL things that I loved about Diane was her big heart for all people. Namely, children, if you haven't already figured that out! There wasn't anything that she wouldn't do for children. For example, while we would be out running errands or whatever, if she saw a child in need, she would go over and begin to take care of them.

This would happen even if the parents were only a few feet or even inches away! I would constantly have to remind her that they have parents. When I did, she would just have this "I can't help it look" on her sweet face.

In anything she did, she put her whole heart into it, no matter how big of a challenge or what the cost. If she believed in it, you were either with her or not. And if you were of the latter, it was just best to stay out of her way. I always chose to be with her because I knew and understood her heart. Mostly, this was for the simple reason that it was always connected to mine.

My middle daughters' friend would spend a lot of time at our house. Usually just hanging out, doing girl stuff, and not to mention the occasional sleep-over. She was very sweet and seemed happy when she was at our home. We eventually met her father, who was the parent that had full custody. He seemed okay, but when he was near her, I noticed that the girl's body language and demeanor would change into a tense state, and had an almost fearful way about her.

Our time with the girl was pretty consistent. One day, things got very real. I had come home from work, and began my walk up the pathway to find my daughter, and her friend, sitting on our front steps.

Both of their faces had a very serious and troubled look on them. They wanted to talk to Diane and me, so I called Diane to see if she could leave work a bit early and told her something big was about to happen with our daughter and her friend, and I needed her here.

When Diane showed up, we stayed outside, and things began to unfold in a very unexpected way. I will not go into detail, but we were told things that no one ever wants to hear of happening to a child. Hearing the issues just lit Diane up, as well as myself, and Proverbs 31:8 was sounding off loud and clear: *"Speak up for those who cannot speak for themselves."*

This wonderful girl, who I will nickname here Number 5 since we already had four children, needed someone in her corner. We said, "Send us LORD." From that point on, and after jumping through many, many various types of hoops, we ended up with Number 5.

Now, Diane and I had often talked about becoming foster parents, but way after our kids had left the nest. We never thought it would happen this soon! I guess God had other plans for that thought. Much later down the road, I came up with a saying, "One comes, one must go."

The kids weren't sure if I was kidding or serious—I kind of liked it that way, if ya know what I mean! If you want to talk about growing pains (which, by the way wore on everyone), there were many, and some we hadn't even thought about. I can't tell you how many times that I would go to Diane totally distraught, wanting to send her back into the system like she was some kind of defective item I was returning. I'm not gonna lie, it was hard for me, and I know it was hard for Diane — not to mention what Number 5 was having to deal with. If I really were to push the issue of wanting to return her, I think Diane would have gone along with it— although, under much, much protest.

I know in my heart that I would not have been able to complete the task set before me if it were not for the strength and presence of the Holy Spirit or without Diane.

At one point, our youngest looked at us and asked if we could keep her as if she was some lost, stray puppy! We all had a good laugh at the cuteness of that. As God would have it, we did keep her! After a few years, the time came for her to be able to enter the field of adoption. Up to this point, we were her foster

parents. Our day in court had finally come. All of the T's were crossed, and all of the I's were dotted.

As we stood before the judge, she went on to speak of how we were to recognize Number 5 now. She was saying, overall, that because we have made this commitment of permanency and added her to our family, we were to treat her as an equal heir and afford her all of the same rights as all of the other blood siblings have within the family.

It was funny to me that she said such a thing because that is exactly how God treats all of us once we become adopted into His kingdom. Galatians 4:5 tells us, *"... to redeem those under the law that we might receive the full rights of sons."* Verse 7 goes on to say, *"...and since you are a son, God has made you also an heir."*

Honestly, neither Diane or myself needed a judge to tell us that stuff. We wanted her to be a part of our family and already considered her our daughter. We loved her. But even better, she wanted us too! Besides, once you have three, a fourth and a fifth kid really doesn't make that big of a difference, does it?

There were many shenanigans that ensued along the way, including a few boyfriends and school dances.

Cheerleading was in the mix, and Diane and I went to many of the football games because of that. Plus, our oldest boy played on the varsity team. We also added a few more bike rides to solve all of the new issues that arose because of a new dynamic in the house. But not to worry, we were able to come to many solutions because we were *still* working together as one.

I can remember one time when Number 5 was accused of doing something to another student in high school. We all got pulled into the principal's office that day along with one of the counselors. Have you ever heard the saying, "Don't mess with mama bear?" Diane was that way with all of our kids. She was professional when needed to be and a down right grizzly mama bear when it was needed too! I was really glad to be on her team.

But it didn't matter, right or wrong. I was always on her side. My love for Diane grew even stronger, and we drew closer together than ever. By this time, we had quite the little empire going. When we all showed up somewhere, people knew who was in the house! What a great feeling that was.

It wasn't long until it was time for Number 5 to graduate High School, and we were wondering what she wanted to be when she grew up. The survey said: COSMETOLOGIST! She was our daughter and was to be afforded all of the same rights that the rest of our flock had.

Diane and I sat down with her and helped her figure out how to make it happen. One of the many things that Diane was really good at was figuring out how to come up with the funds to support our kids in accomplishing their dreams, whether it be a college or a trade school of some kind. I would panic a little, and she would tell me calmly that we could do it.

All the while, I'd be looking into her beautiful blue eyes where all I could do was shake my head yes. Did I ever mention that she had the sweetest face? Squirrel! Not all of our kids were able to follow through with college or trade tech school, but all of them have flowed into doing things that they love doing, and if I say so myself, they are quite successful.

Number 5 has grown into a beautiful young woman, and her career has blossomed over the years to become very fruitful. She now has a family that is growing as well.

We are very proud of all of them and happy to be able to see how they continue to progress in life.

All of this incredibleness happened because Diane and I took a chance a long time ago and followed our hearts. Sometimes I think about how different things might have been for the kids and how they may have turned out if we hadn't taken those chances. They always talk in movies about time travel, and that if you ever go back in time, you can't mess with anything, or else the future could have catastrophic outcomes for everyone.

So if any of y'all are thinking about traveling back in time, remember, don't... touch...anything! Mainly because I don't want the life I have had up to this point to be changed one bit.

Diane had a unique way of helping me to stretch my heart. Even when I didn't want to, she made it happen. It wasn't in a forceful way, but mostly by way of example. Number 5 was one such example. I didn't think I had it in me to take on a stranger's child and love them as my own. But I soon found out that I could because of the heart that Diane had for those who could not speak for themselves.

She had a very special relationship with Number 5 as well as with all of her children.

It's rare to come across someone who is, as we say, a natural at whatever the task may be. But, she was a natural at being a mom. Also, she wasn't half bad at being a wife, either! At times, we hear from smart people that we shouldn't put people on such high pedestals because there may come a time when they could fall off of them. I'm here to tell you that I agree with that statement. Although, I don't think that it means we shouldn't admire or think highly of someone.

I know we are not perfect human beings (for there is only one who is perfect), but there still needs to be a certain level of respect and, most of all, unconditional love for someone—especially if it's the one that God has blessed you with to spend the rest of your life with. To me, She was simply amazing—and I know her kids thought so as well. She never let us down.

With the addition of each child, we were both blessed beyond what our hearts could handle. Number 5 was no exception, and she brought our family to another new level of existence and to a greater understanding and feeling of love.

Our family unit couldn't have been more blended if we had tried. I think that's what made our group so special, was the fact that we weren't trying. It just happened! I have never seen anyone so adept at handling all of the stuff that would get thrown at us on a daily basis.

Diane was seamless and almost never skipped a beat. I, on the other hand skipped many beats. But seeing her in action made me want to be better and do better at everything in my life, including being a father.

CHAPTER 6

The Open Door

Luke 11:10 "For everyone who asks receives; the one who seeks finds; and to the one who knocks, the door will be opened."

EARLIER, I TOUCHED VERY BRIEFLY on where we were in our walks with the LORD—so let me go into a bit more detail. This was something that we went through together, that was an incredibly beautiful experience, and I will treasure it forever.

Diane's father was Irish Catholic. Therefore, she was raised Catholic. The church that was attended was in Burbank, and is still there and thriving to this day. I had been there a few times in the past (before Diane and I were together), and I must say that it did offer a sense of peace and comfort as soon as you walked through its doors.

She had her own Bible and rosary beads. In addition, Diane already had faith in God. She may not have been 100 percent committed, but nonetheless, it was there. One quick note: this was the church where she married her high school sweetheart. My time in church as a youngster was not horrible, but it wasn't that great either. My parents had me baptized in a Methodist church as a baby, even though my dad was Catholic. This caused an issue with my dad's side of the family; they wouldn't come to the baptism because it wasn't a Catholic church. My parents went through with it anyway. As I got older, my mom decided to try attending the same Methodist church where I was baptized. She seemed to like it, but for me, not so much.

You see, I would have to go to the kid's Sunday school class taught by Methodist clergy, aka nuns. The kids were very unruly, and the sister never had any control over the class.

In turn, she would always end up having to call for the other minister on duty to come in and put the fear of God into us to calm down! I can honestly say that I was not one of those little demons in the class. Mom would ask me how it was, and I finally told her what was happening in there and that I didn't want to go back.

She honored that request, and we soon became Easter & Christmas church peeps. The one thing that I fully believe now, as I spoke of in the beginning, is that God's prevenient grace was working in our lives and moving Diane and me in a direction towards each other and towards Him. So now you have a few more pieces to the puzzle of our young spiritual life. If I haven't already touched on it, or even if I have, let me just make it clear: I know God wouldn't ever bless or want an affair to happen.

But He most certainly blessed our lives together once we made things right both as a married couple as well as individuals with Him.

Skipping ahead to our time as a married couple, we began to attend a church where we felt comfortable, as did our kids. Like us, they had some friends that went there too. Remember when I was telling y'all about my park church and how broken I was and how I had given in to whatever the LORD had in store for me? Stay with me here because I want to share something with you.

One Sunday at church, communion was being served. For months, I never walked up to take communion, but Diane always did. I could see the look on her face of not necessarily disappointment. Still, one of hope every time that day would come and go while I would remain in my seat until one Sunday it happened.

Things just seemed different, and I heard one of the pastors that served there explain it to me one day in a way that it all just finally clicked for me. The next communion Sunday came, and guess who went up with his wife? Me!

If you could see the look on Diane's face that day, it was as if she had just won a big jackpot or something.

I think back on that day now and realize that was the day I had caught up to her in our walks in faith. We were finally, and completely, equally yoked. God did it again.

Soon, God began working on our hearts, and we decided that we needed to serve in some type of ministry and not become the family that sits in the back and hides every Sunday. So we asked around for suggestions on where to begin this journey.

Seems to be that if you're not sure of where God is calling you to serve, but you know that you should be serving, it's best to start in children's ministry. So we did, and it was quite an adventure.

We became very active in the AWANA ministry, which is like Christian Boy/Girl Scouts, and would meet every Wednesday night at the church. There would be over 200 kids and adults running around that place!

Diane and I started out as team leaders, then moved on to being directors, camp directors, and eventually, COMMANDERS! That's right—the head honchos of everything answering only to God and the Pastor that would oversee that ministry.

During those wild nights, we would provide the music for song time for the various age groups as well. In addition, God called us to form a Blended Family Ministry. We later became coaches for softball and baseball teams that the church would sponsor. We even had a cheerleading squad that would show up at the flag football games, where Diane was one of the coaches!

Pure craziness ensued, but we had a blast, and I loved serving in ministry alongside my best everything, Diane.

Prior to Number 5, our entire family had gotten baptized one Sunday. It was the first time that the church had ever done a baptism for an entire family. We took up the entire service! It was a very exciting and blessed day, to put it mildly. Mind you, this was the same church that we were married in.

Our time there lasted for a little over ten years, and during that time, I was beginning to feel a strong call to serve in music ministry and to break away from children's ministry. When I decided to let go and let God, I was soon directed to a small church just down the street from the one we were attending. A good friend of ours was serving there and needed my help with music for their children's Sunday Christmas program. Of course, I said yes to her and to God.

This little church happened to be in transition between a lead pastor and a worship leader. Then I walk in! After the program was over, I was approached by the church secretary and asked if I would be willing to fill in while they looked for someone to take the worship leader spot. Well, that was a no-brainer for me, and my answer was a resounding yes!

I was eventually asked to stay in the position, and I happily accepted their offer. Meanwhile, we hadn't made a total commitment to moving our attendance to the new church because we still had kids that were happy where they were and with being around their friends.

I would have to leave that church early and then drive down the street to the little church to lead worship. Then, Diane would grab everyone and drive down the street to be with me at that church.

As my duties and responsibilities became more involved there, Diane and I had a decision to make. To leave our church home of ten plus years and to fully commit to our new place of worship was a move of faith.

We grew a lot spiritually at our home church, and I will never forget the times we had there and the people we got to know. The old friends, and the new ones, will be forever in our hearts. However, our kids still wanted to attend church there, and we tried that for a while. They were getting older, and their priorities began to change. It wasn't the direction Diane and I were hoping for, but it eventually happened.

Life, and ministry life, began to really take off from this point. I'm not saying that we were not 'in it to win it' at our home church, but rather saying that things

stepped up a notch at our new home. Once again, I had my best girl singing with me, and we were making music for God.

Our worship team was small, but we sounded bigger than we actually were. Rehearsals were on Wednesday evenings, and then church service was at 10:30 Sunday mornings. My heart was full watching and listening to Diane sing; her voice only got better with age.

Sometimes I was so taken by her sound that I would forget where I was in the song. Just to see the joy that was on her face to be able to sing for the LORD was something I'd never experienced before—it was truly genuine. Now, our kids did go to the new church for a while, and during that time, the other folks were trying to figure out our family dynamic.

You see, three of our kids didn't have my last name. I didn't adopt them because I wanted them to stay with their bio-dad's last name. The other two did have my last name as well as Diane's, of course. I think they were all calling me dad at the time, and this was just throwing everybody off kilter.

It was very funny to see the looks of contemplation on all of their faces. You could almost see the wheels just turning inside their confused minds. At some point we did explain it to everyone, and then, almost in unison, a sigh of relief fell over the room as if you could audibly hear everyone say, "Ohhhhhh, That's why."

Being considered a blended family was not the way we interacted with each other. Instead, it was always as if we were all blood-related.

The reality for us was that there were no step-children or adopted children (other than for legal reasons). They were just simply our kids...my kids.

There were many exciting things that happened within as well as outside the walls of this new little church. Diane went on to co-lead a women's Bible study. The word got out to their friends, and soon there were women from other churches attending. These ladies had it going on every Tuesday night. I had the privilege of being the Pastor that would oversee that ministry. Oh, did I just call myself Pastor? More on that later.

The music ministry put on a few evening concerts as well as putting together a children's concert. Folks, let me give you a small piece of advice; when God opens a door for you to go through, you need to do it! As the song says from that old school claymation Christmas show, "You put one foot in front of the other...". Listen to what the Holy Spirit is prompting you to do, and if it's the wrong thing to do, you'll know—trust me!

One of my favorite things to do with Diane was to get together and share with each other what was going on in the various ministries that we were involved in. We were able to bounce things off of one another, brainstorm, problem-solve together, and do that in regard to our family needs.

Our time together was moving along fast and furious. And we came to a point where we felt that we needed some time away together to plan, organize, and set goals for the new year that we would be facing.

I had a full time job as a merchandiser (as well as being a Pastor), which made me what's called "Bi- vocational," and one of the areas I would have to cover would take me into Santa Barbara on occasion. On the way back one day, I noticed this little cliffside inn. I stopped to check it out and thought it was perfect for what we wanted to be able to do.

When I got home, I shared the brochure with Diane, and she loved it! We then made that our place to go during the New Year's Eve weekend. It was sort of a spiritual/romantic weekend getaway, all in one. And since we both loved the ocean, well, let's just say, it was a little piece of Heaven on earth for us!

This trip would happen almost every year, if not more than once. It was one of the few times where my girl could totally relax and release all of the yuck that was clinging on to her. It almost felt like we were kids in love again. Oh, and let's not forget that we brought our bikes! We would go on little adventures in and around the area, including Solvang, Santa Barbara, etc... But the weekend always went by way too fast. It was a great tool to help us prepare and focus on the new year and its challenges both in ministry and personally—at least the ones we knew were coming.

Sometimes not much work got done there but instead would turn into more of just a weekend to refresh and restore ourselves. Those times were very special to me for many reasons, and nothing was going to get in the way of that! Diane and I continued to grow closer together both in ministry and in love—our bond was unbreakable. Just when I thought that we couldn't have become any stronger, like we were at our peak as a couple, God would bless us and fortify us even more than ever thought possible. Yes, there's more of this coming.

The reason I say this is because God kept on providing the opportunity for more doors to be opened and walked through.

And I must be honest with y'all. These callings were not anything I would have thought of in the slightest.

Diane and I arrived at the little church in December of 1999, with maybe a week or two left in the year. We had been serving there about two years or so before the new Pastor started talking to me about the possibility of getting ordained. This was something that was the furthest from my mind for many reasons. Heck! I always wanted to be a Park Ranger, not a Pastor!

Some time passed, and Diane and I talked about it, prayed about it, and even went away for a weekend. We eventually came to a decision, and it was yes. Remember, when the Holy Spirit is working on you about something, you must listen and follow! Our new Senior Pastor and now dear friend guided us through the process until a comment came up about things that had happened in our past.

One comment was that Diane was a divorced woman, and being raised Catholic, let's just say that at the time, divorcées didn't have much love coming their way. The second issue was dealing with how we came to be together. In our minds, that could have been a deal breaker. But something very surprising and unique happened with the denomination and its stance on such matters.

I spilled the beans to our Senior Pastor, and he was very understanding but wasn't sure how the higher-ups would see it. We were then tasked with having to write out an official statement documenting the events that took place, leading where we were today. Needless to say, we were stressing big time! This sparked another weekend away. But this time, we ended up in the mountains at a Christian camp with separate cabins for pastors to use for free.

As always, we prayed about it, talked about it, and then prayed some more about it. The two of us worked hard together, and Diane took the reins that weekend by being the designated writer of our beginnings on how we came to be.

When we got back to town, we presented our statement to our Senior Pastor, and he then brought it to the District Superintendent, who then shared it with a few trusted board members.

After this, we met with a couple of board members and were asked a few more questions. Finally, a decision to move forward was made. I was very impressed and happy with this outcome and asked what made them okay with our rough start early on.

Their answer was amazing. They said it was because they looked at where we had been, the things that we had been through, where we were today, and the fruit that our lives together have brought about along this journey.

Just as God has forgiven our sinful behavior, so has the church followed God's word in a beautiful and grace-filled manner. Without further ado, off to the races we went!

We decided what path to take, and it was the one of becoming an Elder (Reverend) in the Church of the Nazarene. There was a course of study I had to complete, in which there were a total of twenty-four college classes to take online. I am not much of a student, but I dove in wholeheartedly just the same.

Guess who was by my side the whole way through this? My girl, as always. Now mind you, she would support me in any and everything that I wanted to do, good, bad, or ugly. She was right there with me. This meant that sometimes extra household duties would land on her to give me the time I needed to write a paper or to get an assignment done on time. The reason it took so long for me to complete the course of study was that we had a family and full-time jobs to deal with.

There were so many times I would be trying to study or work on an assignment, and I would have trouble focusing.

It came to me one day to call my wife. She would answer the phone at work, and I could tell her my issues, and she always had something to say to me that would talk me off the ledge and get me back on track and refocused. Like so many times before, I could go to her for anything.

Even if she said nothing, it was still okay because I knew she was there for me and if nothing more, she listened. But the best thing she would do was to pray for me and, in real-time, with me, over the phone. I remember often going to her and sharing with her all of the new things that I was learning about and all of the things that God was revealing to me.

We even got into a few intense discussions when it came time to unlearn what we thought we knew to be true. I don't think I could have gotten through all of this without her devoted love and support. What's more, I probably wouldn't have been there in the first place if it wasn't done with her by my side. It wasn't just me taking those classes/She took them right along with me.

She suffered along with all of my frustrations and struggles, including when I would doubt myself and question my worthiness to continue in this direction of becoming a Pastor. During this process, she would continually lift me up in prayer and constantly tell me how proud she was of me. Little did she know just how proud I was of her. I was married to a Proverbs 31 woman before I even knew what that was.

After my ten-plus years of schooling, it was time to get grilled before the credentials board. These were the people who would decide if you were ready for ordination or not. Around a large table, Diane and I, with our Senior Pastor, sat with about fifteen or so men and women. We were sitting at one end of a very long, intimidating table.

I remember one time Diane said in jest, "Why do I have to go and get grilled? This is your deal!" Of course, she came along willingly. She had to be there anyway to complete the interview. All in all, we not only survived it but we were approved for our ordination!

Ordination night was intense but spectacular.

There were other ordinands that evening, and when it came to our turn, we knelt down while the higher-ups would lay hands on both our heads and begin to pray along with many other pastors on the stage. Our Senior Pastor led the way, and the rest joined in. I was ordained on June 22, 2012, but I feel like we both got ordained that night.

We were always good ministry teammates, but she became a pastor's wife this night. There was that look I knew and loved on her face again, filled with joy and love.

One of my daughters is a police officer, along with one of my nephews. As mentioned before, Diane's father was a retired police detective. Upon attending our daughter's graduation from the academy, I noticed a Police Chaplain sitting on the stage along with all the other brass. And whammo! God threw open another door. I was about to become a Police Chaplain!

There were many open doors that happened along our walk with the LORD. Diane and I went through them all together. Some panned out, and some got pushed aside, and we were redirected.

These events I'm sharing with you now were two of the most significant ones affecting our spiritual lives.

Once again, to become a Police Chaplain, there were more interviews, questions to answer, background checks, live scans, psych evaluations, and waiting. Fortunately, for this time, all of it was only on me.

I don't recall Diane having to do anything for this one other than her be the woman she was for the man I was. It may not have been as climactic as Ordination night was, but it still carried a lot of, dare I say, pride with it. I had the honor of becoming a Police Chaplain in 2013.

If I've said it once, I've said it a thousand times...I really love seeing that look on Diane's face—it *never* gets old.

Right about now, you might be wondering what Dianes' big accomplishments were in life. They were things that didn't come with a certificate or a badge and uniform. They didn't come with some extravagant ceremony or public recognition.

In fact, some of her greatest achievements were never even acknowledged. Only those who were close to her and really knew her knew what she had accomplished. There was no glitz and no glamor.

Diane's successes were the conquests that meant so much more to her than any of that other stuff. She gave life to four children and took on another as her own, creating a family. She loved me unconditionally, and at times I know it was hard for her to do (*wink*).

Diane was the main breadwinner in our home, which allowed me to have a somewhat lesser income, and for me to go after certain goals and achievements as mentioned before. There were endless sacrifices she made.

She served God fully in various kinds of ministries, as well as being the best friend that she could be to others. Her sense of balance with all that was going on was unmatched, and she would often have people asking her, "How do you do it?" Her reply would come from James 1:22; *"Do not merely listen to the word, and so deceive yourselves. Do what it says."*

I always tell my worship team that we sing for an audience of one. Meaning that no matter how many people show up to the church, whether one or a thousand, we were there for the LORD—our audience of one.

My girl lived for an audience of one. And for her, all she really wanted when it came time for the trumpets to sound was to hear the words, *"...well done, my good and faithful servant"* (Matthew 25:21). She was a blessing to many, but most of all...to me.

CHAPTER 7

Parents

Ephesians 6:2 "Honor your father and mother..."

IN THE NEXT FEW YEARS, a storm began to brew, and the seasons were preparing for change in significant ways. These changes are those that no one ever wants to talk about or have to go through—but still, they come.

Diane's parents were still with us and still married to each other, going on fifty-plus years! My parents were also still with us, but they had been divorced since I was four.

All of our parents were still living independently, while my mom was living in our backyard in a very cute little granny house, which she designed and then built. I don't know of too many spouses that would allow something like this to happen. Diane didn't skip a beat when this needed to be done.

As I said before, I'm an only child, and my mom's relatives were either too far away or had already gone up to glory, so it was up to me to do the right thing. And as usual, my girl was right there with me and unwilling to let me go through anything alone. She loved my mom, and they had known each other since the days of Love & Laughter.

Mom was still pretty independent and didn't need anything like twenty-four-hour care, but it was nice being close enough to help her when needed. We had wired up an intercom system for her, so all she had to do was push a button, and we'd be there in a flash!

On the other hand, my dad was a different story for a while. He was living with his common-law wife for many years, not too far away from us, and we would visit him/them almost every Sunday with the kids in tow. They lived in a townhouse that had a nice pool, and the kids would come over in the summer and go swimming.

They loved him and he was crazy about them. Diane's folks had a house also not very far from us. It was the same house that Diane and all of her siblings grew up in. This house was really cool because not only did it have a pool as well, it had a basement! You don't see too many of those in Burbank. Many family parties and holidays were spent at their house, and we had a blast.

Her dad had these two cars that he kept immaculate and garaged at all times. One was his work/stuff hauler, which was an S-10 Chevy Blazer. The other was a beautiful older model Cadillac. It was baby blue with a white vinyl top—so cool! One of the most unique things I've ever seen was these fly traps that he had made. I'm not sure if they were his idea from the start or not, but they were something.

What he did was construct this frame out of wood that would be lined with a fine wire mesh screen. The bottom section of the screen had a funnel-like opening that as it got raised up inside of the frame, it would get smaller. Once the fly flew up the larger opening, it would have a much harder time trying to get out of the smaller one. The problem now was that you needed some bait, and here is where it gets weird.

The main missing ingredient was dog poop! That's right, you heard me correctly. He would gather up a small pile and place it under the trap for fly bait, and Voilà!... that thing was full of flys. They really helped keep the flys away from the food when we had family swim parties. I wasn't sure if he was a genius or just nuts! Her folks were awesome. We both had some pretty cool parents in our lives, and though they weren't perfect (who is)? they were definitely engaged in our lives growing up, and we surely knew that they loved us.

Because our parents were mature in years, it can't go without saying that they all were dealing with some kind of health issues.

For a long time, various medicines were keeping things on an even keel, and life was cruising along as well as it could for all of them. I had lost my grandma in 1986, back when Diane and I were just good friends. It was a sad time for me because my grandma basically raised me since my mom was a single parent and had to maintain a full-time job that kept me sheltered, fed, clothed, and involved in every activity under the sun! However, the possibility of losing the people we love hadn't really hit me that hard until the 2000s.

Diane's father had a few health problems, but the one causing him the most trouble was his heart. They tried different things and meds, but these were really just a bandaid in place of doing what really needed to be done. We all were spending a lot of time over at their house, not only because we were helping dad, but we were also helping mom because her illness was kind of overlapping his.

One day, a call went out to everyone to get to mom and dad's house ASAP! By the time I had gotten there, he had already graduated to be with the LORD.

Fortunately, others were there with him, so he wasn't alone as he passed away in his home. It was in March of 2003. This was a time that launched a run of lost loved ones that didn't seem to let up. This cycle went on, and it would span over the next twenty years or so.

It was for sure one of those times when you look up an asked God, "What are you doing?" among other questions I'm sure that would come to mind. Almost one year later, in April of 2004, another call rang out through the airwaves. One of Diane's older sisters had three children. One girl who is beautiful and smart, and two older twin boys who are handsome and very talented in the arts. Both of them were musicians and had even started a band at one time, and they were pretty good too.

It was one of the twins.

He had been battling some very tough and unrelenting demons in his life and was using various means to do so. But after so many attempts to overcome the battles, to him, there was only one way left that would allow him to escape the suffering that he endured. His brother found him, but it was too late.

I realize that he was not one of the parents as the chapter is titled. Nonetheless, this young man was a big part of our family, and the loss was a great blow that added to our perpetual heartache during this time span. We all loved him dearly.

Diane's mother was a very special lady. She not only was married to a cop (you had to be special to handle that occupation), but she also gave her husband five beautiful children: four girls and a boy. I now understood where Diane got her motherly instincts from.

She was a block-mom. A block-mom is a mom that would take care of every and any kid within a one-mile radius. That included having them over to her house to go swimming; giving them lunch; just hanging out; letting them use her house for a game of block hide & seek, and then doing all the patches and repairs for any and all cuts, bruises, and skinned knees. She was trusted and loved by the other moms and by their kids. Children were safe when they were at their house.

I don't know how she did it but she had a very calm and peaceful nature about her amongst all of the chaos. Her voice was never raised, but everyone knew when she meant business.

She was the glue that held the household together. Various health issues attacked her body, but the big ones that took their toll on her the most were Parkinson's, her heart, and Dementia.

It didn't take long for all of these issues to get a foothold inside her, even though she fought hard. We soon reached a point where she needed round-the-clock care, so the family did what they did best and jumped into action. There was no question in anyone's mind (mine included) that we would do whatever needed to be done to provide care for her.

Diane would take a nighttime shift a few times a week and took our youngest along with her for a sleepover at grandma's house. I would stay home with our other children and make sure they were taken care of while she was gone.

Eventually, it got to the point where we needed to have professional home-care step in, and what a blessing these ladies were. They seemed to love her almost as much as we did!

I'll never forget when Diane and I brought her to our church one Sunday, and the Pastor was preaching a message, asking us, "If Jesus came for you today, would you be ready?". Her issues affected her speech greatly, but there was no question about what she was saying to the world that day. The question was presented at about the middle to three-fourths of the way through his sermon when without any hesitation, she stood up with her hands raised high and gave her answer: she was ready! In March of 2005, Jesus came and took her home.

After both of Diane's parents left us, only mine still remained. My dad was this little Italian guy who stood about 5 foot 3 inches, on a good day! He was full of you know what and vinegar; very feisty. I was taught how to play sports, and often he would try and teach me the ways of the world. Because of the divorce, he was able to have me every other weekend and sometimes a little extra throughout the year. He loved me, and I knew it.

Dad was quite the character, and he was a blast to be around. Everyone loved him. My dad didn't have very good luck with women and often made it known how he felt towards them. He didn't seem to trust anyone of the female persuasion except for Diane. Many times he would just show up at her office and talk to her about his troubles and whatnot. He fully trusted and loved her.

As a child, my dad would smoke one to two packs of cigarettes a day, beginning at the age of eight. I guess that's what you did as a kid in those days growing up during hard times in Boston.

Thankfully, he wasn't a drinker like his brothers were, or else there would have been other issues to deal with, I'm sure.

Later in life, he survived a heart attack at a fairly young age (late '50s) and tried to quit smoking numerous times but to no avail. The years of smoking finally took their toll on his body. They would later turn into COPD (chronic obstructive pulmonary disease) with advanced emphysema.

He also battled diabetes, high blood pressure, and high cholesterol. But it was diabetes that would land him in and out of the hospital, coupled with life-threatening breathing issues. What made it difficult for his treatment was the fact that the steroids to help his breathing would, in turn, make his blood sugar spike extremely high.

The medical teams that took care of him had the unique task of balancing all his meds. He was tough, a real fighter. Soon, the time came when he needed more care than his life partner could handle. She was just as tiny as him and came to us for help.

Remember, I'm an only child and his family lived all the way across the country. Besides, they were not in the greatest shape either.

There were a few people who were a bit closer, but still not in any position to offer any type of considerable help.

The week just before Memorial Day weekend, my dad was in the hospital and getting ready to come home. It was at this point that Diane suggested that we take him into our home and care for him for whatever time he had left. I didn't really know how to respond to such an unselfish, heartfelt act. We were all still feeling the loss of our other family members, but that didn't stop her.

Diane not only was helping to take care of my dad, she was also taking care of me by doing so. I knew she loved my folks, but I knew that she loved me enough to be able to recognize the anguish and the pain in my eyes as to what to do. She understood me like no one else ever could have.

We came home and began shuffling things around the house while he was still in the hospital. There wasn't much time! His new room got painted, wallpapered, and even a chair rail was put up, all done by my girl and me.

We were also informed that hospice needed to begin. He was closer to glory than we thought.

In about two days, we got his room in order and hospice hustled to get all of the necessary medical supplies delivered and set up. This included an oxygen unit, an adjustable hospital bed, a walker, and other various items that would be needed.

It was amazing to see how fast everything came together. The time came to bring him home, but he didn't know he was coming home with us yet.

As we walked into his hospital room, I bent down and said to him, "Dad, you're coming home with us." I don't think he understood what that meant at first, so I made it clear that he was coming to live with us. Y'all should've seen the smile on his face, complete with a little giggle. At that point, I think it was safe to say that he liked the idea.

Here's a good laugh for you. Picture this; My mom was living in my backyard, while my dad has just moved into our front bedroom, and they really still don't like each other much! Go figure!

Anyway, we brought him home on that Friday of Memorial Day weekend, and he soon settled in. There were a few mishaps and shenanigans that took place but he enjoyed being there and he was happy.

In May 2008, on the same weekend, and mind you, he had only been with us for three days, my dad peacefully fell to sleep and began a new journey.

The rest of the family rushed over to be with us as we all did for Diane's mom and dad. There was nothing but love that encircled us that day, and smack dab in the middle of it all was my one and only: Diane.

I called my mother 'mommy' and this was mostly because I called my grandma mom. I'm not really sure how that happened — it just did. The house that I grew up in was in a great neighborhood with great neighbors. Most of them were elderly, but they were really cool.

There were two houses on the lot; the front house was the smaller of the two, the back house was larger, and the one we all lived in. It also had a basement where mom (grandma) stayed. We rented out the front house, but eventually, mom would live in that one, so it would be just my mommy and me in the back house.

Anyway, my mommy was a little thing, all of 5ft 2in and 110lbs soaking wet. But don't let her size fool ya! She was also a typical mama bear. Mommy worked hard to maintain a good and clean household, not to mention that she held down a decent job that supported us all. By this, I mean me, my mom (grandma), and her.

And let's not forget the pets that needed care as well! Now, some of you may know of or remember the 1971 earthquake. It was a big one! It hit early in the morning, and we were all still in bed. Once it started shaking my mommy came flying out of her bedroom and was trying to make it to me. I remember seeing her bounce up and down in the hallway, moving back and forth as if she was on a ship in rough waters. It was quite a sight to see all of this.

Her only goal was to protect me and as soon as she got close enough, she dove on top of me to shield me from whatever might have fallen on me or from any flying objects. It was a little scary, but we all survived and didn't ever get back to sleep because of the many aftershocks that occurred. Regardless, my mommy protected me no matter what. She was willing to sacrifice all for me, and she did.

As a kid, she was rather sickly. She had developed a very bad case of asthma. Back in the thirties, medicines and technology in the medical field were nowhere near what they are today. Because of that, she almost died quite a few times. I guess God had other plans for her life.

There was a time when a major medical breakthrough was about to happen regarding the treatment of asthma but the new drug needed test subjects. Her doctors always had my mommy on their minds and offered it to her for free.

Unfortunately, as much as it may have helped her breathing, it was also causing many unknown long-term problems for her. Her eyesight was worsening and she developed dry eyes as well as cataracts.

Luckily for her, she had some very good doctors that took a genuine interest in her to help her get through these tough times.

However, those tough times ended up becoming worse. Fast forward to her now living in our backyard in the granny house.

Heart issues soon began to be a problem and low blood pressure was a great challenge for the medical teams along with her breathing struggles—she was in and out of the hospital many times. One night she had called us for help and Diane and I went racing across the yard and found her in a bad way, probably the worst one yet. We helped get her ready, and even though she didn't want to go, we went to the hospital.

After spending some intense time in the ER, she eventually ended up being transferred to the ICU. Standing there in her room, I had to make one of the hardest decisions I have ever had to make. The nurse that was in the room with us, with tears in their eyes, looked at me and said that I was her hero, but I sure didn't feel like one. That night in November of 2009, would be the last hospital run she would ever have to make.

There were many times when our parents would bless us with little pearls of wisdom, and I can't help but think of that saying, "If I only knew then, what I know now." That's because now I understand those little pearls much better and would have taken the time to hear them better.

Folks, our parents, your parents, and all parents are an untapped fountain of knowledge, experience, and love that we sometimes didn't or wouldn't engage with enough. I miss them and the times we could've had with them. They were the reason we are here today and part of the reasons why we are and who we are today. One of Diane's sisters said, "We're all orphans now."

I never really thought about being such because we were by then all older and were much into our adulthood at this point, but it's something to think about.

Now that we are now much into our adulthood, I had a sort of grim thought that I shared with Diane. That was the fact that we are now the ones next in line. I know what you may be thinking, but silly things go through your mind when life-changing events happen to you.

Please don't worry, cause you'll be happy to hear that I didn't dwell there for long. During this time, there were other family and friends that we'd lose along the way, which were just as heartbreaking to experience.

We're not going to be here forever, so we better be on our game and not waste any time. We don't know the time when Jesus will come for us, but like Diane's mommy: be ready!

These events, although expected, were still difficult to bear at times. But one of the most comforting things about it all was that Diane and I had each other, and we were strong that way. In addition, we were even stronger together in Christ Jesus. John 16:33 *"...In this world you will have trouble. But take heart! I have overcome the world."* Amen!

CHAPTER 8

The Emerald Isles

Psalm 119:105 "Thy word is a lamp unto my feet, and a light unto my path"

AFTER OUR FOLKS had all passed and the dust had settled, as in most cases, you were blessed with an inheritance of some sort. Our parents were no different in that way. Both of our parents blessed us with the fruits of their labors from the many years of hard work and most of all, their love for us, their children.

Diane and I began discussing what to do with what we had received, and of course, we decided to do the responsible thing and put it all into a retirement fund. But then I had another idea. You see, neither of us had ever been on a really big trip, and by big trip, I mean traveling to another country kind of big trip. I presented this idea to her to use some of the inheritance for such a trip, and she became very excited about the idea.

The only problem now was figuring out where we wanted to go. I have Italian heritage in my bloodline, and she suggested possibly going to Italy. But my girl had Irish heritage in her bloodline, and I told her that maybe we should go to Ireland— I actually really wanted to go there! She said yes, and I soon started my quest to find out how to make it all happen. Since neither of us had a clue as to where to go in Ireland, I first went to the most obvious place to begin my search: The Auto Club of Southern California of course!

It was there that I purchased one of their travel books about Ireland. Upon opening it, I quickly became overwhelmed with all that it had to offer the traveler. I then looked for a map to help me see where we might want to visit, one that actually helped a great deal. At that point, I got online and searched for an Irish travel agent.

I found a company called Authentic Ireland Travel and contacted them. We were very blessed because the agent that was assigned to us was awesome in helping to plan our trip, which was called, "The Romantic Escape."

We mentioned to them that we didn't want to be locked into a tour group where you had to move when they said to do so and only go where they take you. I felt very brave and was willing to drive the roads of Ireland on the wrong side of the street and on the wrong side of the car. What an experience that was, and I'll share more on that later.

Honestly, it was one of the best decisions we made regarding this adventure since it added to the excitement and beauty of Ireland. I felt like we got so much more out of it than having to rush through the land. That was something I didn't want to do because this was definitely going to be a once-in-a-lifetime event.

I had been in contact with our Irish travel agent both by phone and through many e-mails. She coached me through the steps that we needed to take for everything to be in order. She even sounded Irish when she typed! It was awesome!

This was our first time ever getting passports, which was quite an experience. We bought clothing that would prepare us for the ever-changing weather as well as a new camera to take lots of cool pictures: over 600 to be exact! Another important tool that I felt was needed was a dedicated GPS that allowed me to download sections of other countries into it.

This was a great low-cost investment and came in very handy. However, I still needed the help of maps at times because the places we were trying to get to didn't have address numbers. They were just listed by what town they were in. I would look on the map to find an intersection and then input that into the GPS. It worked!

As time grew closer, we became more and more excited to go to Ireland. This was something wonderful for us to look forward to. After a few modifications to the original itinerary, we landed on a schedule that seemed like it would work for what we wanted to do. As I said earlier, we weren't sure where in Ireland to explore, so we ended up choosing to travel through the southern parts, which happened to be more woodlands and countryside, plus lots of places for walks on beaches, both at the ocean and lakes. It was beautiful!

Diane and I really like those types of areas, so this was perfect for us. When all was said and done, we were ready to go on one of the greatest adventures that we had ever been on. We had our passports, proper clothing, and the right technology, complete with the correct electrical adapters. We received our travel packet that had everything in it that we would need once we arrived in Ireland. All we needed now was a ride to the airport.

Here is another one of those times where you really see who your friends are. Our flight out of LAX left at 8:30 AM.

In 2010 people needed to be at the airports three hours ahead of take off. That meant that we needed to leave our house in Burbank by 4:45 AM to be there within the required three-hour cushion. So guess who offered to take us? It was our Senior Pastor/friend. That's right, he offered before we could even think about asking him. It was a great load off of my mind knowing that we didn't have to worry about transportation to LAX!

The beginning of our 600-plus pictures started when we arrived at the airport. Our plane left at 8:30 AM, and we arrived in New York at 4:59 PM. We boarded our international flight at 6:30 PM and landed at Shannon Airport in Ireland at 5:50 AM on September 11th, 2010.

You heard me—September 11th!

I was a little nervous about our date of arrival, but it was a great start to our wonderful adventure, and there were no hiccups to have to deal with, including any issues with lost luggage.

We were both a little tired, but the excitement and the mild adrenaline rush kept us moving and focused. As soon as we grabbed our luggage, we were off to the rental car agency. Here is where the real fun begins.

Since the car was part of our Romantic Escape package there was little that we had to do to get the vehicle. The gentleman that took care of us was very nice and explained all of the guidelines for the trip. Come to find out, there really weren't very many. He knew the area we would be heading through and told us to not worry about getting any scratches on the car and that they expected them.

Diane and I looked at each other funny while the CSR had a little grin on his face as if to say, "You'll see what I mean." Off we went to find the car, and as we approached it, I noticed it was quite small. It was fairly new, with low mileage, but small. There was barely enough room for us and the luggage! But it did get good gas mileage and we made everything fit. So we got in and began to drive to our first destination: Adare.

All of the accommodations except for one were these very cozy and welcoming Bed & Breakfast type houses. The owners of every one of them were extremely friendly and trusting. Upon arriving at one of the houses, the owner was not available to greet everyone because they had to run an important errand with one of their kids. There was a note left on the entrance to the house that had the names of all who were arriving with the room number next to it, and the keys were on our beds! You won't ever see that here!

The couple at our first B&B in Adare greeted us, and we chatted with them for a while, then they showed us to our room. Diane wasn't feeling so good, but it wasn't too serious that a nice nap wouldn't fix. Afterward, we decided to explore a little, so we took a walk around the area. I was walking in Ireland, holding my best girl's hand. She had colored her hair at the time to a stunning shade of auburn and this combined with her gorgeous blue, sometimes hazel eyes and fair skin. Well, let's just say that her Irish was really showing on her.

As for me, the Romantic Escape had begun. My wife looked absolutely beautiful. By the time we got back to Adare Country House, dinner was served, and then we went off to our room.

After a good night's sleep, our adventure continued, and we were on the road to Kinsale. It was kind of a harbor town and was also the only place we stayed that wasn't a B&B. Many little shops, restaurants, and pubs lined the streets, and all were within walking distance from our hotel, called The Old Presbytery. It was too very comfy and cozy.

Diane and I weren't really sure where we wanted to eat so we decided to eat everywhere. We had appetizers at one pub, salads at another, and the main course and desserts at a different spot. The colors in these towns were amazing because almost every building and front door was painted a different color, and they were all right next to each other as if they were one building.

When we walked over to the harbor area, I noticed something unique. Maybe it was just me but after I said something, Diane noticed it too. It was the fact that the ocean water had no ocean smell to it as it does in the states. Here in the US, you know when you're by the ocean.

But in Ireland, not so much. It didn't matter though, because the scenery was so pretty, and the company made it even better.

One really cool place we visited was called Cobh. If I remember correctly, it was the last place the Titanic had stopped to pick up some folks just before it set sail on its final journey. There was a lot of history at that spot, and my girl wanted to know everything there was to know.

What's more, Diane could remember all of the information, unlike me on the other hand, who was just as happy to take a bunch of pictures, as I did!

The Jameson Irish Whiskey factory was also close by and, well, we couldn't be that close and not do the tour. It was really fun! Fota House was also on our hit list and we were glad we went. It was a huge property, and I mean HUGE! Fota House was absolutely gorgeous. The grounds went on forever and everywhere you turned was something more beautiful than what you just saw.

I would have hated to be the gardener for that place! There were many people there that day, but you wouldn't have known it because the place was, dare I say it again...HUGE!

Best of fall, it was close to water where we found a trail that led to it.

We sat there for a good while, just taking in the peacefulness of the area and just enjoying being together. While on our way back to the main area of the grounds, I spied with my little eye this giant beetle. But there was something different about it, and had to take a closer look to see what was going on with this bug. As luck would have it, this thing was carrying a piece of, how do I say this politely, animal dropping to its home. And yes, of course, I took a picture of it!

We spent about three days in Kinsale and then it was time to move on. Even as we were driving to our next location it still seemed like we were already there. The whole countryside was amazing and beautiful to see and every mile we drove felt like just one giant experience as if there were no gaps in our trip. As we were driving, we went to Blarney Castle, and yes, we kissed the Blarney Stone. The grounds were beautiful and we spent some time walking around them and seeing many different types of plants and trees.

I couldn't resist taking some silly pictures of both of us while in those trees. You could almost feel the history all around as it was happening. Not only could you walk through the castle, but you could see and walk on the Battlements that were used during the conflicts that took place there.

The old watch towers were still present, and we were able to go in them. It was like something you only would see in a movie, yet we were there! One of the areas in Blarney was very sweet, and we happened to be there at the same time they had their annual little carnival, and I do mean little.

But that's what made it so sweet and hometown-ish. Families were out together and enjoying life in its simplest form. I'm not gonna lie, but it kind of made us want to live there.

After we woke up from our fairytale village visit, we left there and finally made it to our next B&B in Kenmare, which was called Annagry House.

At this time, I would like to share with you one very special part of our driving experience.

Remember when I mentioned that the car rental agent told us not to worry about getting any scratches on the car? While driving through the countryside (which was basically the entire trip), we soon discovered why he wasn't worried. As we were driving down this beautiful, but very skinny country road, we come to pass a sign saying, 'Beware of Gigantic Farm Equipment.' Diane and I looked at each other again and were trying to figure out just how gigantic these vehicles were in reality.

Well, it wasn't long until we had a first-hand look at their size because no sooner did we see the sign than we came face to face with one of these behemoth farm tools! It kind of reminded me of those huge super dump trucks that have tires the size of your car. It truly was gigantic and green, I might add. As it got closer, I began to panic, wondering what I was going to do.

There was no room to pull over to get out of its way, so I did what any good safe, driving husband would do.

I immediately began to hug the left side of the road which totally shoved Diane's side of the car into the gorgeous shrubbery that lined it. And I might add, to my expert driving abilities, I didn't miss a one! (Recap; I'm driving on the left side of the road on the right side of the car.)

When we returned the car at the end of our trip, there were quite a few scrapes on the side, and as promised, nobody said a word.

This happened a few more times, but by then, I had become a highly trained professional in the art of avoiding gigantic farm equipment and in taking out all shrubbery that was near the roadside!

All the while, Diane had total trust in my skill level, even though she may have let out a few squeals and whimpers now and then. In any case, we arrived in Kenmare unscathed. Once there, we headed for a place called Muckross Traditional Farms.

These grounds contained original, maintained buildings and various areas that were conducive to farm life back in the day, just before the introduction of electricity. If you ever thought about living off the grid, well, these people definitely did exactly that, and it was not done by choice. We walked around the entire place, and one of the best attractions for us was the animals that were in their pens and corrals.

If I hadn't mentioned it before, Diane absolutely loves pigs! And guess what they had there? That's right...piggies. There was even a mama pig with little piglets, which just sent Diane into a frenzy!

We were at that pen for a while because we were able to reach over and pet them. For Diane, this was a little bit of Heaven. For me, the same was true, but for different reasons, because I knew how much she enjoyed that time with them, and I was with her.

Although we were only in Kenmare for two days, we still managed to find the beach, which like many of us, is our happy place and especially when it's in another country.

We parked the little car and walked on Ireland's shores, collecting seashells and holding hands. We found a really quant little beachside cafe and had lunch—what a perfect day. As hard as it was to do, we were able to put the problems and responsibilities of life back home on the back burner for a while, while we enjoyed this almost fairytale adventure and the chance to be finally able to just be us.

As we journeyed on to Dingle, or An Daingean (which was the official name at the time) we couldn't miss an opportunity to drive through the Ring of Kerry. It was a beautiful drive, but something special was happening that day. There seemed to be some sort of bicycling event that involved large groups of road bikes riding for the day.

As luck would have it, during our lovely drive through the Ring of Kerry, we began to come up behind a group of riders. And then another one, and another one, etc... As we traveled onward, the groups would start becoming larger. This meant that with the roads already extremely thin, and the constant threat of gigantic farm equipment ever present, now we had to deal with bicycles that wouldn't let you by.

Occasionally, you would come up on a nice group that would let you pass through. We were moving along nicely at one point, and I decided to pull over and take in the view as this route was along the cliffs overlooking the ocean. It was a great place to stop, but our peaceful and romantic gazing didn't last for long.

For what did I see approaching behind us on the distant horizon? There were more bicycles! I yelled to Diane to hurry up and get in the car! She was wondering what was wrong and looking at me like I was some sort of a crazy man.

I immediately filled her in while running and digging for the car keys, yelling, "The bicycles are coming...the bicycles are coming!"

Don't laugh at me! You guys don't understand how hard it was to navigate around those folks trying not to hit one of them!

I could just see the Irish newspaper headlines now, "Irish Cyclists Taken Out By Crazed American Driver From California. He Was Trying To Beat Them To The Finish Line!"

But just in case you were wondering, we did make it out before they caught up to us—it was quite the drive, but we conquered it! There was one more obstacle we faced that needs to be mentioned.

It's called rush hour. Now, in Ireland, this meant something very different from here in the states. It still had to do with traffic, but it was a different kind of traffic. You see, the farmers in the area had many sheep, and they would often make their way to the roadway where the vehicles would travel. It wasn't just one or two; it was a whole flock! The flock would come onto the roads and travel on them for a while until they found the right turn-off for them and then simply disappear down or up the side of the mountain.

While on the Irish roads, rush hour traffic would then take place and the sheep couldn't care less! It was just part of living in the countryside of Ireland. I must admit that this was one of the few times that rush hour traffic didn't bother me one bit. I felt blessed to have gotten to experience it in this way. Besides, it didn't matter to me if our roll got slowed because my girl was there with me, and it was all part of the adventure.

Rush hour soon cleared up and the bicycles were left in our dust and we breached the little town of Dingle to check in at Dunlavin House. The area that this B&B was set in was amazing, just like all others.

The view from the house overlooked a small cemetery, but it wasn't a creepy cemetery. It just seemed to fit the area perfectly. In addition, the backdrop to the cemetery was a large inlet-type body of water that was lined with mountains on the sides which funneled into the bigger part of the ocean.

After we got settled there, we went to explore the famine houses. This was quite a sight to see, and we were impressed that some of these homes were still standing. Some of them were more like a big one-room shack that wasn't very well insulated. But those were hard times, and people were trying to survive as best they could.

There were even some old photos available that showed the sad faces of those who were having to experience such an event.

It was very interesting to see and learn about the history of another country. Sure, we learned about things that went on around the world in school and all, but it was different when you're actually there, walking on the same pathways that they walked on and stepping into the homes as they may have done so many times before.

During some of our adventures while in Ireland, it would rain off an on, and I could swear, that if you stuck out your tongue, you could almost taste their tears. Thankfully, they were strong, resilient people, and they are still here! PTL! We explored An Daingean as best we could because we were only there for two days, but they were still two wonderful days.

We made our way out of the gigantic farm equipment danger zone and rush hour/bicycle invasion, which signaled that, sadly, our trip was coming to an end as we headed north towards Bunratty.

Bunratty Castle Mews was to be our last B&B. This was also near the airport we were going to be leaving from, which was located in Shannon. I must say, that the owner of this B&B was quite the character but not in a bad way.

Personality was definitely one of her strong points. She was a little thing but full of spunk, complete with leopard print yoga pants! There was a castle to visit when we arrived, called Bunratty Castle.

You could walk the grounds and in the evening they would put on a type of period musical entertainment show, with full costumes and food from olden times.

Mead was the drink of choice long ago, so that was served, which neither of us had ever tried before. All I can say about the mead was that it was different. We also got to experience one of Ireland's oldest pubs, called Durty Nellies. This historic pub was established in 1620! I think it was there that I made friends with a young man playing the piano, and I'm still in contact with him to this day! What a treat!

The show at the castle was reminiscent of the one we have here in Buena Park, California, only it wasn't as action-packed or rowdy. Still, it was a very fun evening, and it rounded out our time in Ireland perfectly. After the show was over, my girl and I wandered through the gift shop area and eventually went back to our B&B.

The next day, we had our last Irish breakfast, headed to the airport, and turned in

our brush-burned car. Everything had run super smoothly until we hit the customs section. The customs agent asked us a few questions, but one stood out more than the others. She asked us if we had any contact with farm animals or had any sea shells with us. I'm not sure exactly why it was an issue there but it was.

Pure panic went through my entire body as I looked at Diane, knowing full well that we had done both, and quite extensively, I might add! Our answer was: Nope!

If they had only looked at our 600+ pictures of us loving on just about any farm animal that would let us touch them and seen us collecting shells on the beach, we probably would have been in quarantine for the next year! Luckily, we managed to snow the customs lady and we got through to our flight.

Looking back now, though, I kinda think she knew differently and didn't want to hassle us. Thank you, Irish customs lady!

There were many things we saw and adventures we took that I didn't mention. For example, we must have hit every woolen store in every village we drove through. Diane was having a field day in them. I swear it was like watching a shark feeding frenzy once she walked through the doors. But I didn't mind because she was happy and that's all I cared about. Besides, she looked really nice in those woolen items, so I actually benefitted as well.

We explored many more points of interest and national parks, which also gave us the opportunity to pet the wildlife. There were many beach and forest walks and multiple pub visits! Like I said, everything about this trip was perfect, and I do mean everything.

After we got back home, we were on a high for about the next month or more—it was all we could think about and talk about with each other. It definitely was one of the best decisions that we had ever made, and we felt so blessed to be able to take this once-in-a-lifetime adventure. For quite a while, it felt like we had only been back a few weeks when in reality, it was a few years! The time that we shared there together in Ireland will stay with me forever, and I will continue to hold on to those memories for dear life.

However, some things do tend to fade, yet the important stuff always remains. Just knowing that we were in such a place together and in love made it all the more magical.

CHAPTER 9

What Comes Next?

Acts 1:7 "...It is not for you to know the times or dates the Father has set by his own authority."

MOST OF US WILL SPEND TIME making plans for the day or even for the future. Sometimes that works out for us...but then there's God's plan. And as we all know, that usually doesn't coincide with ours. Nonetheless, those of us who are faithful will obey and change course as required. Those who don't will continually wonder why life is so hard and so much work.

I'm not saying that you won't ever have any problems; I'm just saying it depends on how you handle them.

After our trip to Ireland, Diane and I began to feel the need to do more family vacations. You know, the ones that we all would remember in the years to come—the epic adventures!

So what did we do? We bought a motor home! That's right! A regular RV! We soon began making plans.

Before Number 5 came along, we had planned one of those epic adventures to Yosemite. We ended up going there with another family we were good friends with through the church we were attending at the time. The mom was a nurse, and her husband was an officer with the LAPD, so we traveled with them, their children, and our entire family.

Diane and I loaded up our tenement on wheels, and we headed out to see sights unknown, looking forward to exciting new experiences! We all arrived without a hitch, mainly because we left so darn early that the kids slept most of the way there.

I didn't know how much of a blessing that really was at the moment until we left to come home. Our living quarters on this adventure was a three-walled, tin roof, tent concoction that had a broken-down enclosed wooden fence, that created a small yard space. It was really useless in keeping anything or anybody out. But hey, we had an LAPD Officer with us who brought his off-duty weapon: what could possibly happen?

We settled in quickly. Diane soon got to work looking over the brochures to see what we could find to explore. Hiking was the obvious thing to do. So the next day, my lovely wife and I took our kids on a hike. The area was beautiful this time of year because all of the mountain and forest flowers were in full bloom.

Oh the colors, oh, the many smells, and oh, the pollen!

We took off down this path that put us right in the middle of it all. Then it began. It hit me all at once. The sneezing, the itchy burning eyes, the running, no, gushing nose. Diane and the kids continued on because I had become overtaken by the alien life force that dwelled in the disguise of lovely flora.

Diane was laughing so hard at one point she was unable to help guide me out as I could not see through all of the puffy eyes, the tears, and snot that covered my face! One of my kids asked her, "What's wrong with dad?" She lost it even more.

I eventually made it out of "Meadow 51." But all in all, it still was a great day. Night came, and it was time for dinner. We ate but of course, we had trash to deal with. There was a trash can, but this was no ordinary receptacle. These had to be bear-proof trash cans, a very important detail. I had forgotten to put our trash in them just one time. That night was an all-out war with the wildlife around us when attack time began at 4 AM.

I was awakened to find a 300-pound bear digging through the trash I forgot to secure. I think I surprised him as much as he surprised me. My poor Diane was wondering what all the ruckus was about. It was just me shooting the bear in the behind with a halon fire extinguisher that I had brought along.

He took off running and I of course chased him out of the campsite and up a hill. As I was returning to our most unsecured dwelling, I came face to face with what seemed to be a 9-foot raccoon who was headed straight for the trash that the bear was just enjoying! It goes without saying that he got lit up with the fire extinguisher as well! By the way, I was a dead-eye with that extinguisher.

There were more run-ins with the fauna but nothing that me an Ol Red, couldn't handle (insert tobacco spit). Maybe it was from lack of sleep, but I swear I thought I saw the Bald Headed Bear from the movie "The Great Outdoors." We had many cool adventures and saw some awesome wonders of nature while visiting this historic park, but all too soon, it was time to go home.

As usual, Diane took care of the inside of the motor home, and I took care of the outside. By the way, we weren't allowed to sleep in it per park rules because we weren't in the motor home part of the park. Anyway, we started our trek down the mountain, and all of us were wide awake this time.

All of a sudden, someone began to feel car sick.

You can only guess what happened next. One kid started, and then a chain reaction occurred that made Pompeii look like the beautiful water show outside the Bellagio in Vegas! Our oldest boy used one of his sister's shoes while blankets and pillows were being destroyed—it was pure mayhem. For some reason, nobody ever thought to try and get to a sink or the bathroom! Remember, I'm not a poop and puke guy... I'm okay with blood and guts.

I had that motor home pulled over and stopped in record time, and I was out of the vehicle running down a path that I had found not too far away, barely escaping with my life. It was a very traumatic experience for me, so stop laughing!

I left Diane alone to deal with that mess because, in some weird way, she understood. Don't judge me!

Again, I think it was the same kid who asked, "What's wrong with dad?" way back in Meadow 51 that also asked, "Where's dad?"

I had disappeared so fast that no one knew where I was!

All I could hear when it was all over was Diane's sweet voice calling for me to come back. Things got tied to the rear bumper and placed in outside compartments after SPEWNADO had finally passed. We had about six more hours to go, but we made it home unscathed the rest of the way. PTL!

Next on our list planned for a re-model inside the house.

Our kitchen was okay but very dated, and space was not used very well. Plus, I wanted to give my girl a new kitchen to work in comfortably. She was good with that idea too!

We contacted a family member that was a contractor and asked if he would be willing to take on such a task as he was very busy because he was very good at what he did. He said yes, and off we went designing and planning colors and appliance relocation.

Shopping at the local big box hardware store was almost a daily event. Luckily, we were blessed with the right people in our path to make this project happen. It was so much fun to go shopping together and I really treasured those times. Shopping had become a type of therapy for us because we were almost constantly battling issues with our kids or ministry challenges. Strangely, it really helped a lot!

Items were ordered, supplies were bought, and work had begun. My oldest son was into demolition work at the time, so he even pitched in to help along with Diane's brother.

Everyday when Diane would come home from work, a little bit more of our house became revealed and mangled—but all of this chaos was necessary. I think the

best part about the re-modeling was that Diane didn't have to cook very much at all. You see, all of the electrical, water, and gas lines to the kitchen were disconnected. So I ended up doing a lot of BBQing!

Fortunately for us, my kids had bought me a really cool grill for a past Father's Day, and let me tell you, it got put to the test. The BBQ and I survived, and I had a great time cooking for my family.

At this time we had a cat named Whiskers. I must say, he was the best dog I ever had! We would let him out to roam his neighborhood (yes, I said his neighborhood) and I could go out at night and whistle a certain way, and he'd come running from a few houses down the block to come in for the night.

When Diane would come home from a long day at work, he could tell the sound of her little truck and would come and sit at the curb where she would park, wait for her to come out, and then walk with her to the door and into the house.

Mind you, I'm allergic to cats. So you ask yourself, why does Bill have a cat? Well, funny story. So quite a few years prior, we were living in a different house. It was the one that Diane and the kids were already in at the time before I moved in.

My oldest daughter had a friend down the street where their cat had kittens. She had decided to bring one home. I, of course was against the idea but decided to give it a try. At the time we were painting the living room, and all of the electrical socket covers had been removed.

One night while in the kitchen, Diane and I see this half-grown ball of fur dart across the floor in that same room. I went running to see what the fuss was and in his mouth was a mouse! The mouse had come through one of the openings in the wall that was missing an electrical outlet cover.

That night he earned his way into a new home and our hearts.

During the remodeling, there was a very big hole in the floor that was big enough for a person to crawl into.

We didn't know it at the time, but Whiskers had stroke-like events. He decided to jump down into that hole that led under the house, and most likely, it would be his final resting place. At first, we didn't know where he was. But through my expert sleuthing, I discovered where he had disappeared to.

So I did what any good father would have done and sent my 6ft. 2-inch 300-pound son down that hole to recover our little boy!

He ended up finding him, but after that incident, he didn't last too much longer (talking about the cat, not my son)! At least he passed with dignity and not under the house—we miss him very much. There were many other pets that we'd lost along the way, and they all had something very special about them that would keep them in our hearts and memories forever.

The re-modeling was coming along nicely and with minimal setbacks and snafus. When it was finally completed, it was time to reveal Diane's new kitchen to her. I should have taken a picture of the look on her face while seeing the end result, which was priceless.

It turned out amazing! I wanted so badly to give her things that I hadn't been able to give her in the past.

This kitchen was something special for her and something that I could give her at the time. It was worth it, and it was one of the ways to show her that I loved her for all of the sacrifices that she had made for all of us throughout the years.

One of my favorite artists growing up was, and still is, Kenny Loggins. Diane had found out somehow that he was playing at a "Concert in the Park" series, and it was close by.

We decided to go since it was almost Father's Day. Some of our friends, along
with their kids, ended up going with us and we made an afternoon of it. What a super time it was. However, my kids had a special scheme in the works.

My youngest daughter took it upon herself to nab one of the programs and began a totally full-on assault on Kenny Loggins to get it autographed for me for Father's Day. He did it of course, without hesitation, because who could resist a sweet little blonde-haired, blue-eyed girl? I mean, c'mon! She not only had him sign it, but she went back a second time to have him add Happy Father's Day to it! This kid was something else!

Our oldest boy decided on a different approach and in Ninja fashion, snuck his way to the front of the crowd and was just in front of the stage. He then began taking some really cool pictures of Kenny and the band. By the way, the very expensive camera that he was using belonged to our friends who didn't realize that he had lifted it for the mission! I even got my picture taken with him!

The whole day was amazing, and what made it that way was that we were all together. You don't realize how much you miss those times until they're gone.

There were a ton of other adventures that we all experienced to include: beach camping trips, theme parks of all types, desert camping trips that involved dirt bikes and quads, a Grand Canyon trip, fishing trips, family parties that involved the entire family, and finally, all of the various holiday celebrations that would happen throughout the year.

We also enjoyed the countless ministry events that we all served in together.

God saw it fit for us to have these experiences and we loved every moment of them! It goes without saying that we had a very busy life together—I wouldn't have had it any other way.

Being by Diane's side was the best adventure of them all! Because of her, I did things and experienced things that I probably would not have ever given a second thought.

My life had become so much fuller with her in it because her life was already so full. She literally gave me all of herself and never held back anything. This included her children, her love, her support of everything that I wanted to do without question. No matter how goofy it was, she always said, "Let's try it and see what happens." But best of all, she gave me her heart, the most precious gift that a man could receive from a woman.

Men, if you ever come across someone that totally and unconditionally gives you their heart, please don't mess around with it. There is power and strength in that gift beyond anything you could imagine. Aside from the love that God has shown us and continues to do, there is no greater gift than the love of a good woman. Don't make her second guess your love for her.

CHAPTER 10

Seasons of Change

Ecclesiastes 3:1 "There is a time for everything and a season for every activity under Heaven."

SOMEWHERE WITHIN 2017 and possibly towards the end of 2016, Diane's health became an issue. Other things had popped up prior, but they were things that were expected because of family history.

For some reason, this particular family inherited affliction grew into becoming something that we never expected it to become. Diane had developed Diverticulosis. I have read that it's something that people might get after the age of 40. Well, I guess it was Diane's turn to deal with this issue. All in all, Diane had been a pretty healthy person without any real major problems.

At a slow but steady pace, the symptoms became more and more intense. The Diverticulosis soon would turn into Diverticulitis. Any of you that know about this problem understand that there can be severe stomach pain, accompanied by fevers that are caused by the infection raging inside you. This issue is not something that you simply take Tylenol and then stay in bed for a bit. Medical attention is needed.

As the episodes got more severe and more frequent, so did our concern about what needed to be done to control them. Occasionally, she would end up in the hospital for a couple of days and then be released to come home. My girl was beginning her long road of suffering.

However, she remained the strong woman that she was, and she didn't want to let this problem hold her back from living life as she has always done: BIG! Once again, it was time for the seasons to change, and it wasn't for the better.

It seemed as if the attacks knew just when to come.

They almost always would strike at the most inopportune moments. Many times we would be out somewhere for the evening or even on a weekend getaway, and she would become very ill and experience great pain. At that point, there really wasn't much to do other than work to keep the fever down and to try and make her as comfortable as could be.

It was an uphill battle, and her life was slowly becoming not her own anymore. As time went on, we remained strong in our faith, and our prayer time increased a bit. We worked harder than ever to maintain a normal lifestyle as much as possible.

Sometimes it worked, and sometimes we had unwelcome interruptions. Now, Diane was usually the one that was what we would call clingy. That meant she always had to be touching you in some way, whether it be holding my hand or sitting almost on top of me if we were watching TV. That didn't bother me.

But during the new changing of the seasons, I soon found myself becoming more and more...clingy.

During this whole process of finding out what to do with the new challenges that had gotten in the way, Diane would have to endure many various kinds of tests and trial and error sessions, hoping to find a way to obtain minimal pain and discomfort. They even had to test to rule out ulcers and bowl obstructions as well as kidney stones and such. But it always came back to being Diverticulosis.

Even though sometimes the testing was not the best of times, to say the least, we were glad that they were being thorough and not simply telling her to take three aspirin and call them in the morning! However, the diagnosis seemed to be correct and on point. This, in turn, told us what we needed to do to try and make the symptoms less painful and more manageable.

Family and very close friends were the only ones that knew of her condition. She received a ton of information on how to deal with this type of ailment. And just like good, responsible adults, we attacked the internet to find out more about all of the other things that would go along with the "D" word.

We must have printed out everything we saw and then some. Soon, we had a three-ring binder full of all kinds of medical and dietary information. Dealing with this disease included a drastic change in diet. I don't mean just cutting out a few things; I mean cutting out almost everything that is near and dear to your heart!

Mostly the dietary restrictions had to do with foods that contained seeds and husks. Popcorn, tomatoes (but okay if you took out the seeds), strawberries, beans, corn, and other foods that might take a while to digest, were no longer allowed for Diane to enjoy. This was not easy for my girl, and she made it known often. I would try to help and remind her, but that would soon turn into anger on her end.

I understood that it wasn't me that she was angry with—it was this dreaded disease that she had unwillingly obtained. Sometimes she would almost seem to give up her dietary intake and just eat whatever she wanted to.

We both knew it would be a bad idea and knew of the possible consequences that could follow. More tests and blood work, along with ultrasounds and X-rays with contrast, were to be constant events in her future from now on. For a while, we seemed to have gotten it kind of dialed in. Even though, at times, she would have a slight flair-up, it was manageable.

I keep saying we because when you are with someone, and you are truly in love with them (at the risk of sounding corny), you really do feel their pain, and you *will* walk through it with them. NOTE: Never let the love of your life feel alone...ever!

Just when we thought it was safe to go back into the water, something unimaginable happened.

Things were cruising along at a *manageable* rate of speed until this one weekend trip we had taken. It was, of course, our favorite place by the ocean. On the way to our destination, Diane was beginning to feel symptoms that were part of Diverticulitis. They weren't the normal gut-wrenching pains as yet. But after we had arrived and spent a little bit of time there, they eventually began to increase in intensity.

Remember, fevers are part of the attack, and she was beginning to spike one. I couldn't tell just how high it was at first touch, but it wasn't at a point of concern. We did the usual routines to combat the fever, which were Tylenol and a cold washcloth on the forehead.

Most of the time, that did the trick, and we were back to doing whatever it was we were doing. But this time, it was different—we couldn't get the fever down.

It kept climbing, and her stomach pains got worse. I decided that maybe we should go home, and she agreed. I never got us home so quickly from this place before, and I was hitting speeds I didn't know that vehicle could hit! One of the issues when driving was that she felt every little bump in the road, no matter how small it was.

I swear that day, I must have hit all of them. We finally made it back home in one piece (PTL!), and I helped her to get in the house and then get her comfy.

The fever was relentless, as was the pain in her tummy. Finally, I reached her doctor to let him know what was happening. He was concerned and said we needed to get to the ER. By now, Diane had slipped into almost a zombie state of mind.

What I meant about her zombie state was that she wasn't responding to my voice anymore. She wasn't passed out, and she was still able to sit up. But her eyes were closed, and to get her to respond, I had to kind of yell out her name, and then she sort of responded back.

I didn't have any idea what was causing this kind of behavior, and I started to become even more concerned than usual.

I was able to get her to walk with me to the truck and had to continue to raise my voice to get her attention; all the while, her eyes were closed. As we approached the ER, I decided to drive right up to the door, left her in the truck, and went inside for help. They helped her immediately, taking her right into an examination room. Everyone had a serious look on their faces, including me.

There was one ER doctor and at least two nurses working on my girl. I answered the usual questions they would ask, and I filled them in on what she had been battling with.

When they took her temperature, a new vibe entered the room, and things began to speed up. I asked what was wrong. The doctor said that her fever had risen to 107!

My sweetheart was burning up! The team started placing ice packs all around her...working very focused on getting that fever down. One of my questions to the doc was, "What happens if it gets to 108?" His reply..." There are no 108 degrees.

The high fever was causing her a zombie state of mind.

Things were very tense for a while, but they were able to get her issues a little more under control, and the fever came down, finally! She ended up staying in the hospital for a few days, and while she was there, her Tummy Doctor (Yes, this is the technical name!) came in for a visit. He then ordered a battery of tests to help determine what he already suspected.

We all know that fevers usually pop up due to an infection in the body. Well, Diane had an infection, alright! The outcome from all of the testing told the Tummy Doctor that surgery was needed to locate where the infection was and to remove it from her.

He explained all of it to us and that it wasn't something new for him to do with people. We knew he was at the top of his field and went along with his recommendation to have the surgery.

The time came to begin the process for this major event. He had explained to us that he didn't expect to have to take out too much of her intestine and it was all pretty routine for people who suffer from Diverticulitis.

I prayed with her, kissed her, gave her a smile, and told her that I'd be right outside in the waiting room —she forced a smile back. It may have been routine for the doctor, but to us, it was a very big deal.

Something strange happened while she was in surgery.

The doctor came out in the middle of it to talk to me and began to explain what he found inside Diane's tummy. He found that an abscess had burst, and the fluid was moving throughout her body which in turn was causing the fever. Also, he discovered that a large amount of her sigmoid colon/intestine was damaged beyond repair and needed to come out—three feet, to be exact! She would have to have an ileostomy bag while things healed up.

The good news was that the bag wasn't permanent. While in the hospital, we were trained on how to manage the ileostomy bag. Then the time came to send us home and begin a whole new adventure.

I can still see her sweet face looking up at me, knowing that poop and puke were not my things. But for her, I didn't think twice.

I would do anything I needed to do to take care of my sweetheart. So, we did it. There definitely was a learning curve and some obstacles to deal with during that time, such as allergic reactions to the sticky tape (another technical term).

I found a solution for that challenge and for many others that reared their ugly heads. It was my girl, and I was willing to fight for her care.

Soon, it was time for the reconnect surgery, and finally, NO MORE BAG! It went very well, and the Tummy Doctor was happy with the way things had turned out.

Although, the Diverticulosis would remain with her for the rest of her life, and her dietary changes and restrictions needed to remain in effect.

The major damage was dealt with, and a new beginning was in her future. Hooray! Hooray! Hooray!

Little did we know at the time that the new beginning we were so excited about was really the beginning of the end.

CHAPTER 11

A Sleeping Giant Has Awakened

Ephesians 6:11 "Put on the full armor of God, so that you can take your stand against the devil's schemes."

AS PER USUAL, time marched on, and our bodies began to change once again. My health had been maintaining a pretty even keel because I was on meds to help me control my various inherited issues. This was a very good thing because I needed to be stable for what was about to come in the way of Diane's health status.

Disclaimer: I feel that it's important for you all to know the events that led up to where things are today and the emotions and feelings that went into all of the challenges that she/we faced together. That is why I'm sharing some of the medical issues to help give you a better understanding of what shaped, changed, and even grew and strengthened my love for her as a husband.

Just one more thing: please forgive me as there were many things happening at once, and the pace had picked up somewhat, so my timelines may be off a bit, but you'll get the picture.

Back to it! I have a hard time sometimes remembering dates and years when things happen. Fortunately for me, Diane really liked to journal. As I read through one of her entries, I came across the date that the giant awoke.

It was in July of 2017 (per her writing). We had begun to notice that she would struggle with doing regular everyday activities in the way of having shortness of breath. Simply going for a walk soon became a big effort.

We would have to take breaks every so often. One of her favorite places to be (if not her favorite) was to go to the beach. One time we took a drive to see the sunset.

We parked and grabbed our beach chairs, and began our traverse over the sand. It wasn't long before we would have to stop for her to catch her breath.

We eventually made it to where we wanted to be, but it turned out to be quite the ordeal. I have never seen my wife look so weak before that day, not for any reason. Like we all do at times, we were trying to think of what was causing such a breathing issue and landed on the possibility of it being asthma.

The doctor prescribed an inhaler which helped a little bit for a little while, but it was not the fix we had hoped for. The sleeping giant had made its presence known, and little did we know at the time, it was here to stay. We needed to prepare for the most important battle of our lives, mainly hers.

More strange and unique issues began to show their ugly heads. The first plague came as a swollen tongue as well as sores inside her mouth. The sores were making it hard for her to eat, and the swollen tongue was also contributing to eating problems, not to mention that it was making it hard to talk without sounding like she had some sort of speech impediment.

We tried every OTC med that we could find to help with the sores, but nothing was really working...she was feeling miserable. The second plague was the disintegration of her finger and toenails. At this point, her primary care doctor referred her to a Dermatologist.

After his initial inspection and battery of tests, he was leaning towards the issue being an Auto Immune Disease.

He prescribed a steroid cream that had zero effect on the nails. The best part of me (which was Diane) was beginning to feel very ugly and unattractive.

I'm sure you all have heard the phrase Natural Beauty. Well, Diane had such a quality in that she didn't need makeup to look beautiful. I always used to tell her, "I wouldn't be seen with no ugly woman!" She would laugh at me and give me a look. Little did she know how serious I was in that how gorgeous I thought she was no matter what. Now, not to be bragging, but I have had some really pretty girlfriends in the past.

But there was something very special about Diane's beauty that went above and beyond anyone else's.

I'm not just talking about the looks (which she definitely had). It was more about her heart and what she did with it (Ya see, I'm not that shallow)! I'm no Brad Pitt, but I definitely married above my pay grade, and I knew it.

She battled with all of her serious issues for a few months while making numerous trips back and forth to different doctors that were trying to figure out what was happening to her body.

During this time, another plague arose in the form of her losing her hair...it had begun to thin out. Little by little multiple strands of hair would come out on a daily basis.

Diane always had a thick head of hair, and I think that helped it not look as bad as she thought it did. But those who knew her could tell the difference. I could see that her confidence and her demeanor were starting to take a hit.

At one point, her primary care doctor decided to send her to a Heart Doctor just to make sure that they were checking into everything. He ran a battery of tests as well; Stress Test, EKG, Echocardiogram, Angiogram, and last but not least, an MRI!

With the results of these tests, her doctors began to lean in a different direction as to what is going on. The center of her heart had become enlarged, and the lower half of it was not functioning efficiently enough.

This was causing fluid to build up and fill her plural sacks around the lungs, causing pressure, thus making it hard to breathe. Her lungs simply could not fill with enough oxygen.

We were soon turned over to a Hematologist/Oncologist doctor. Somewhere in the middle of all of this, the fluid had to be drained (both sides) so she could breathe a little easier.

This occurred a few times and, of course, was a painful procedure. I would sit in front of her, and she would hold onto my hands, and I would let her squeeze as hard as she needed to, all the time telling her to focus on me, and I would remind her to breath. She was a strong lady and made it through. There was a great amount of fluid that would come out of her, and this was surprising as to how much there was, even to the medical staff.

We were usually in the hospital when this would take place, and the doctor that would do the procedure was her primary care doc, who happened to be an Internist/Pulmonologist—it was nice to see a familiar face during all of this. The plural sacks were filling up faster and faster and it soon became evident that there was a need to insert drainage tubes into her chest...one on each side. Up till now, they had to puncture her through her back and go in between the ribs with a very long needle to extract the fluid.

So, another surgery was in the very near future to insert these tubes indefinitely into her body. When she was ready, the time came to leave, and the discharge team came in with all of the instructions for home care, including a training session for us on how to use the

Plurex drainage kits. It wasn't hard but it wasn't something that I had ever done before or even seen.

I paid attention as best I could and even took a short video of the technician performing the routine. I was scared to death that I would do something that could hurt her in some terrible way.

There was a constant concern of infection, and I did my best to keep the area clean and the sterile items as sterile as possible. But as always, it was my girl, and I was ready to do anything to take care of her.

More tests were ordered at the Hematology/Oncology Institute, and one included a bone marrow biopsy that, in the end, revealed nothing. We began to take notes of what the doctors were telling us because there was a lot of info being thrown at us.

I wouldn't say that it was a bad feeling, but the doctor at the Institute didn't seem to be able to provide my girl with the care that she needed, and the doctor that was assigned to us agreed. So if I remember correctly, in 2018, we ended up at Keck Hospital of USC, a 401-bed acute care hospital that's part of Keck Medicine of USC, the University of Southern California's medical enterprise.

This place was a bit overwhelming but also a little bit comforting as well because I felt that maybe, just maybe, something might actually get diagnosed and then treated.

Upon our first visit/consultation, we were introduced to a doctor who was a Medical Oncology Specialist. She was a highly regarded specialist in a particular area, and we were about to find out what area that was. As Diane and I were sitting across from her, she began talking about a disease that we had never heard of before. I'm sure there are many diseases that we had never heard of, but this one was a real humdinger.

AL Amyloidosis. That's right, you heard me correctly.

We came to find out later that there are different versions of this disease, and some of them are curable...but not the one Diane had.

We both had to take a step back for a moment and try to catch our breath when we heard this news. The doctor did go on to tell us about other patients who had this disease and about some of their successes. At the time, this disease was still in its infancy, and not much was known about it.

One of the treatments for AL Amyloidosis was discovered by accident on another patient, and I think it is still being used to this day (more on that later).

Eventually, Diane got admitted and then assigned a room. Looking back, I was so thankful that Covid had not hit yet because I knew I wouldn't have been able to be with her. That would have just totally full-on, literally broken my heart!

Again, more testing and biopsies to help determine and confirm their suspicions were performed, but this time the biopsy was of her heart. It was the one thing that I treasured most about her.

The thought of someone going to go in and extract pieces of it terrified me. I tried not to show my fear, and I think I did a pretty good job. As for Diane, I could tell that it made her a little uneasy too, and rightfully so! The first attempt was a failure because the doctor that performed the biopsy didn't get enough for the lab to test. I wasn't happy, and neither was my girl. But, another attempt was made and this time we had success.

After the procedure was done, on the way out of the biopsy room, they had Diane hold on to the samples. When she was passing by some family in the hallway, she looked up and said, "I'm holding my heart in my hands"... all the while, God had the rest of it in His.

If memory serves me correctly, I believe that the treatment prescribed by the Institute and prior to USC was a low dose of Chemotherapy along with some other medicine in pill form.

We would go in once every couple of weeks and sit in a comfy chair while the nurse would start an IV on Diane.

Remember when I said that this treatment was discovered by accident? Well, they decided that this was the way to go at that time. Even though it was a low dosage, it was still chemo, and it came with all of the popular side effects as well, including more hair loss.

After all of the medical procedures were completed at USC, it was time to go home. I think, all in all, she was there for about a week. We had one final meeting

with the big cheese and was given the news of what all of the test results had yielded.

You know the kinds of tests, I mean; the news that we had hoped we wouldn't have to hear. Like, this disease is not curable, but, as far as they (the doctors) knew, it was manageable, and there is hope for a long life—although it needed to be altered a bit. The doctor also informed us of other options that could offer the possibility of an extended life, which included stem cell treatments, stem cell and chemo treatments together, and even the possibility of having a heart transplant.

Our doctor told us about one of her patients, a female pro-golfer who had come back to about 80% while dealing with Amyloidosis.

It offered little encouragement, but we took it as such anyway. The drive home that day was one of the longest drives I've ever experienced (even though USC wasn't that far from home).

I held my sweetheart's hand the entire ride. We were both a little frightened of what the future might have in store, but neither of us let on to each other that we were feeling that way. I was trying to stay strong for her, and she was trying to stay strong for me. We were just trying to digest what had just happened and mostly just wanted to be home, our safe place.

Diane continued with her chemo treatments through IV and pill form, and I continued to keep draining her Plural Sacks, which were still producing massive amounts of fluids due to the fact that her heart wasn't working the way it should.

Soon, an oxygen tank was provided for home use to assist her in getting enough oxygen into her blood.

Eventually, it came to a point where we were able to have a different doctor at the Institute who was a little more well-versed with this type of medical challenge. The new specialist changed Diane's chemo meds to a pill form only. It was a major change, and Diane had trouble swallowing it because there was still her very swollen tongue and sores in her mouth. Fortunately, she only needed to ingest that massive pill once every few weeks or so.

The minute it was time to take it, I could just feel her little body tense up and agonize over having to perform this task. I began to kneel down beside where she would be sitting, take her hand again, and begin praying with her and for her.

We only focused on her getting that pill down, and for that particular moment, we were in. It worked! Well, most of the time, anyway.

Sadly, the sleeping giant had awakened, and it was barely getting started.

CHAPTER 12

The Snowball Effect

Proverbs 17:22 "A cheerful heart is good medicine, but a crushed spirit dries up the bones."

BY NOW, THE BEAST WITHIN my wife's body was picking up great momentum while on its path of destruction. It was wearing greatly on her spirit, even though she tried hard to hide it. More plagues were introduced to the playing field of her illness in the form of certain findings in her blood work and exacerbated the struggles with her heart function.

One doctor had put her on a potassium pill to raise it, and then another had realized that it was going up way too high.

High potassium levels can cause serious cardiac issues and possible death. Bananas were quickly taken out of her diet, but that wasn't enough. We had to redo her dietary plan once again so as not to include items with high amounts of potassium in them.

It soon came to a point where we couldn't control it at home, and the high levels would land her in the hospital. It was more of an IV fix than anything else, but don't forget that she still had Plurex drain tubes in her chest.

I was able to take care of that for her while in the hospital, although it took some convincing on my part with the nursing staff to let me. Fortunately, though, they weren't familiar with such a procedure and allowed me to do it on the condition that a nurse would be present in the room. That was fine with me, and it made Diane feel much more comfortable. One evening, the head nurse asked if it was okay for her to bring in other nurses that were on the floor to watch me do this. I looked at Diane, and she nodded that it would be okay.

I ended up doing a training session for about five nurses. What a trip that was! By that time, I had become a highly trained professional at it! (Lol!).

Anyway, we did our time there, and the levels came down enough to send us home. The newest issue then presented itself: Diane's blood pressure was too low. During one of her hospital stays, the medical staff was beginning to have great trouble in trying to get her blood pressure vitals.

The decision was soon made to put in what I understood to be a central line in her femoral artery, which would help in getting a proper blood pressure reading. While performing the procedure, her primary care doctor, who knew her very well and had been her doctor for a long time, made a joke that only he could have said.

You see, the nurses and assistants that were in the room were worried about Diane's pain level. But her doctor, with a smile on his face, told them not to worry because she could take it, that she had been through worse.

I guess you had to be there to understand the levity. There were no ill feelings because she knew that he truly cared about her well-being. Although, she did give him a wack on the arm! Very cute.

I would just look at her and wonder to myself, "How is she dealing with all of this?" Because let me tell you, I would have wussed out a LOOOONG time ago! No matter what situation got thrown at Diane, she never ceased to amaze me.

I just wanted to be like her when I grew up.

In the meantime, the doctors were changing her medicine constantly because, as we all know, that's why it's called a practice! If I hadn't mentioned it before, this was a disease that not much was known about, and care was almost a hit-or-miss kind of thing at best. But she endured it at the time.

Over the course of all of her hospital visits, there were quite a few of her doctors who would come into her room, look her in the eyes and tell her that they had learned a lot from her.

Hopefully, knowing that through her suffering she possibly helped someone else, maybe brought her some comfort in all of this turmoil.

The time came to make some tough decisions in regard to her job. All this time, she was still going to work, at least for most of the week. Diane was an office manager in an accounting firm that was owned by our brother-in-law. She worked there for over twenty years and took great pride in that position; and was always giving her best by putting in long hours at the office and by making herself available to her clients 24/7.

She genuinely cared about the business and about the employees that were in her charge (and they knew it) and took the time to listen to them, no matter the issue.

Diane was the glue that held that place together, but her mind and her body were not cooperating the way they needed to.

It was time to hang up her calculator and come home with the plan to rest and rebuild with the hope of being able to return, but that couldn't happen.

It wasn't long before that plan was changed (as so many plans had been before), and soon her office was no longer hers and became someone else's.

She had boxed up her personal items that were used to decorate her office and the photos of those she loved that would remind her of why she was there. There were items that she had placed around her space that would let people know that she had a strong faith in the one and only true and living God and she loved Him. Diane was no quitter by any means, so it was a difficult and sad time. But, she understood that it needed to be done for everyone's best interest and mostly for hers.

My girl's strength and stamina had started to deteriorate more and more because of this disease.

It took a lot out of her to move around the house, so I started trying to do more things for her. That wasn't a great idea on my part because doing so wasn't helping her stay motivated in trying to do things herself, and she said something to me one day. I just wasn't thinking.

There were still many growing pains to endure and many more to come. Her speech was becoming even more of a challenge and not only from the swollen tongue and sores in her mouth but also because of the fact that her lungs were now being squished from the fluid build-up and couldn't expand to get enough oxygen in them.

Because of these new plagues, Diane wasn't able to continue singing on the worship team at our church. Singing was one of the driving forces that brought us together in the first place, and she was no longer able to sing. Singing gave her great joy, and I loved accompanying her. Another heartbreaking decision was made, by her, to step down from ministry activities.

It was just as heartbreaking for me because I knew just how much it meant to her. I loved serving God alongside her, and much of that had stopped. In time, she would stop coming to church altogether. Although, she still made attempts to serve in whatever capacity she could. She was not a quitter!

Here's a side note: God can use you no matter what state of health or physicality you are in—remember that!

Her finger and toe nails still were not growing the way normal ones would, and they increasingly got weaker and thin like paper. This also made them very sharp, and she would often cut or scratch herself. In addition, she would worry about hurting our grandkids when she wanted to touch them, but an emery board was always close by to file down any potential problems.

Hair loss continued, and since Number 5 was a cosmologist, she would come over and try to help cut her hair in a way that made Diane feel good about the way she looked.

Bless her heart. She would bring over certain products that would support hair health, and Diane would try them, for a while. To me, it didn't really matter because she was beautiful no matter what.

In the middle of all of this mayhem, there were more potassium hospital trips and doctor visits of all kinds, and testing and procedures. And then there was the chemo pill. Yes, she was still trying to choke that down and having success for the most part.

After some time, we realized that nothing much was changing by taking it other than the fact that on top of how bad Amyloidosis was making her feel, the chemo medicine was making her feel even worse.

The idea behind this pill was that it was supposed to keep the effects of the disease at bay, thus giving her a chance to live longer than projected if not taken. At this point, the disease was gaining more ground.

I feel it was because of the fact that it took so long to diagnose the illness. It had already dug its heels in too far.

Because of this, another tough decision was then made to discontinue the chemo pill. Diane didn't want to be miserable all the time and not be able to enjoy who knows how many years she had left.

Another little unique symptom from all of this was the random appearance of different sizes and shapes of red patches.

They didn't seem to hurt her, but some of them looked like she either ran into something or someone whacked her. They would show up just about anywhere on her body and sometimes in more than one place.

Her skin had begun to change color as well. It had a slight yellow tint to it. This was something else to aid in her already low self-esteem on how she looked.

During this time her primary care doctor had asked me to keep a record of how much I would drain from her plural sacks, and of her blood pressure. I was still draining her every day on both sides, and there was a lot coming out of her. I would never know when the end was near, but when it got there, I knew it because it was painful for Diane.

Sometimes I could tell and gauge when to stop because I would start to see little bubbles in the drain tube, signaling that it was close to the end. Still, most times, not so much.

There were a couple of signs that were in frames I had found in a popular hobby store, and one of them said, "Yay, you're Home!" and the other said, "Walk by Faith." These were up in the kitchen, and she would see them almost first thing when she came home from work.

Sometimes they would bring a little smile to her face and a glimmer of hope to her soul.

Like I said before: she's a fighter!

Our heads were just spinning from all that had been occurring in our lives. In the meantime, we still had five kids to love and care for, with all of their life adventures happening, plus grandkids in the mix too! They have all provided a different type of reality and were a very nice and welcomed distraction through all of it.

Our now-adult children had been doing exactly what people advise others not to do when something medical comes up: they went to the internet and looked it up!

This information stirred up a world of questions, and for some of them, I really didn't know how to answer, not to mention how to deal with all the different kinds of emotions that would pop up.

They were scared and trying to get a handle on things and make sense of what was happening to their mom. Diane and I did our best to try and keep everyone calm and from getting too stressed out. At times it was a bit of a circus, and I think that there were moments when Diane and I were handling it better than they were. For a while, we were all managing somehow and stayed strong together as a family, aka, the people I call my family.

Diane was still able to manage and take care of herself at this stage of it all with minimal assistance. She may have been moving a little slower and would need more breaks because she would get winded quicker, but still, she was mobile, and that was a good sign.

Seeing her still moving around offered just a little more hope that she would beat this thing and continue on in a semi-normal capacity. I think now of that famous line, "Only time will tell."

Our time together had become more precious to me than ever before. She and I used to really work hard to get some alone time where it was just the two of us with no kids or other people around. Now, I was fighting to get as much time with her as possible, with or without others around.

Also, I was still working as a merchandiser, which meant that I was out on the road all day dealing with many different kinds of people. I was having a very difficult time concentrating on my job. I just wanted to be with her.

By now, you can clearly see the snowball effect that was taking place. It almost reminds me a little of that shtick from back in the day; "Slowly I turn, step by step,

inch by inch..." And, as per usual, there were more doctor appointments, more meds juggling, and the ever-present draining so she could breathe a little better. It was as if we would take one step forward and then three steps back.

One day, more bad news came our way. It seemed to be a losing battle but nothing compared to the ambush that was lying in wait.

CHAPTER 13

Please, LORD...Make It Stop!

Isaiah 43:2-3 "When you pass through the waters, I will be with you; and when you pass through the rivers, they will not sweep over you. When you walk through the fire, you will not be burned; the flames will not set you ablaze. For I am the LORD, your God..."

THEY SAY THAT TIME stands still for no one. This holds true, especially when illness is involved. Diane was becoming weaker and weaker with each new day.

The disease that was pillaging her body had gained more strength, and it was learned that it had become something even more sinister than we could have imagined.

Throughout all of the constant testing and monitoring that was going on, it was revealed to the medical team just what this particular version of Amyloidosis (Amyloid Light chain kind) had on its agenda.

You see, what happens with this disease is that your bone marrow begins to produce a bad protein that gets sent out to attack the organs in your body. It had started with her heart, but now it had moved on to her liver and kidneys. After a while, her liver started holding its own, but not the same could be said concerning her heart and kidneys.

The weakness she was experiencing was soon too much for her to overcome, which changed normal everyday functions.

At this point, she could still make it to the restroom and the shower (that had a seat in it for her) but needed help to get there with the aid of a walker, myself, or a family member.

Thankfully though, there was always someone with her. It was quite a process.

Also, something else had to change that I was not ready for, and I'm sure she wasn't. Our bedroom was on the second floor of our home, which meant that there were stairs...stairs that she could no longer navigate even with help.

I never thought throughout this process that there would be a time when we would not be able to share our room again. My sweetheart's new bed was now a couch that was in our den.

We tried to make it as comfy as possible and didn't do too bad of a job. I would tuck her in at night, tell her how much I loved her, and then off to bed I'd go. It was the longest stairway I have ever climbed.

This was not by choice. Amyloidosis doesn't give you any choices. Then, another new plague inserted itself into the mix of challenges, and that was one that involved her skin.

For you or me, it may take a little bit to break or cut our skin. We can even stand a harsh grab from someone now and then.

But for Diane, her skin had become paper thin. Anything abrasive or if someone would grab her, it would immediately not only cause her great pain but also would tear her skin. There would be a deep slice along wherever you had touched her, and it became an open wound that needed care.

Diane had moments when she would still try to help you while you were attempting to move her, and she would maybe lose her balance or begin to wobble a bit. Well, what's the first thing or instinct that we all have when something like that happens? You grab that person's arm or hand, or whatever. Needless to say, she ended up with many open wounds on her at first.

Remember, I was Blood & Guts, meaning I had no problem dealing with those issues.

I can't tell you how bad we all would feel when those injuries would happen. We got better at it, but some mishaps were not too bad, while others were really awful.

I can remember this one horrible time that happened on my watch. We had just gotten to the hospital regarding another potassium issue, and she was in her wheelchair. I stopped for a split second and turned around to look at something.

And then I heard her trying to scream my name: Bill!

I swung back around, and not realizing that the sidewalk was at a slight pitch, she had rolled off the curb and was trying to stop herself. I made it to her and kept her from flipping, but the damage was done. The skin on her arms was like someone had taken a cheese slicer. I fixed her wounds the best I could, and we continued on through the doors of the hospital.

Words could not describe how horrible I felt for letting that happen. She, of course, forgave me, but I could not forgive myself.

During this time, various family members on Diane's side, including our kids, would come and stay with her so that I could still continue to go to work. They would show up early in the morning and stay until about 2 or 3 o'clock in the afternoon.

I can't tell you how much comfort that gave me, knowing that she was safe and in good hands. All of them were like angels for her and for me.

On the home front, another new and unexpected challenge presented itself: COOKING! That's right! This is one area that this dad/husband wasn't very well-versed in, and I'm not afraid to admit it. When the kids were still little, mom would say that dad was cooking, and that meant, what did you want on your pizza?

I was a master at the art of phone orders.

I can do eggs of various types and even got a bit creative with breakfast tacos.

However, you can only eat so much pizza and eggs. I did venture out somewhat and got a little braver eventually, but mostly, I would rely on my phone ordering skills. One of Diane's favorite places for me to get dinner from was Outback Steakhouse.

My baby was a genuine Meat-A-Saurus! Sub sandwiches were also on her top10 of dining masterpieces. But her most excellent all-time favorite dish was prime rib —rare! (Yuck)

It wasn't long until eating became an even greater chore for Diane. As much as she wanted to, her mouth wasn't letting her, coupled with a new plague of having trouble swallowing.

This made it difficult to eat life-sustaining foods and caused problems when it came time to take her meds.

Diane also had developed an intense sensitivity towards anything spicy in nature. There were foods that I couldn't detect any hint of spice in them, but she could. This quickly narrowed her menu to Mac & Cheese, Corndogs/Hotdogs, and soups.

At times she would feel brave and try something different, but it would end up in failure, and then she would feel terrible for making me go and get something that she couldn't eat.

I told her one time that I didn't care if all she ever did was just smell it, and that I would get her anything she wanted.

It was my little way of trying to make it seem okay for her, and sometimes it worked... while others times, not so much. My favorite person in the whole world was deteriorating right before my eyes, and there wasn't anything I could do to stop it. As 2019 rolled around, and with the limited menu that Diane had adopted, she was noticeably losing more and more weight.

Her hair was almost completely gone, and her wardrobe had changed drastically to that of loose-fitting yoga pants and baggy T-Shirts. Doctor visits were becoming harder and harder for us to go to because it was difficult for her to travel.

But this one thing seemed to spark her drive and will to live: Number 5 was getting married! Diane's goal was to walk down the aisle (with some assistance of course) and be seated where the mom would usually sit.

Being the pastor in the family, I've been blessed to be able to do a few weddings for our large family.

This time was different because Number 5 didn't want me to marry her off. She wanted me to be her dad and walk her down that aisle.

This was something I didn't see coming, but I welcomed it wholeheartedly! The bigger challenge was praying that Diane would be able to make her goal of walking down that church aisle.

As time grew closer to the wedding date, we needed to find a dress that would work for my sweetie. The color was to be a navy blue that was long like an evening gown type of feel. I jumped online and began the research. She liked three dresses that I picked out but it was still difficult to know for sure without trying the dress on.

So what do you think I did? I ordered all three of them. When we received them, she tried them all on, which was a chore in itself. We zeroed in on one that fit really well and was easy to put on. It was really pretty and had a lot of lace on it.

I had mentioned that Diane had these gorgeous blue and sometimes hazel eyes, and whenever she wore anything close to those colors, well, let's just say there was never anything ugly about her, for she was utterly stunning. In my eyes, she could never look anything but beautiful, and I was proud to be seen by her side.

The next challenge I faced was her hair or lack of hair.

Number 5 jumped into action and began the search for a nice wig. They looked at some models in various catalogs and landed on a style. When it arrived, she put it on her and worked her hair styling magic. By the time she was done, it had looked awesome on her!

We were getting closer to Diane meeting her goal, and as she put it, "Nothing was going to keep me from walking down that aisle." Diane worked very hard to keep a positive attitude about the wedding adventure, and I soon made reservations at a hotel close to the venue. It was a beautiful day for a wedding, and it was outside, and finally, the moment of truth had arrived.

The game plan was that our youngest son would be the one to walk Diane (mom) down the aisle while our oldest son was sort of off to the side, which would put him close by with the wheelchair in case there were any mishaps.

Number 5 and I were in line behind them and watched every step she took. It was almost a bigger deal for me to see her make that walk than the wedding itself! The smile on her face was absolutely priceless. She was so happy that she was able to make it happen. Then, it was Number 5 and my turn to take the stroll, and we did, and I gave her away.

After the ceremony, there were the usual wedding photos, but at that point, my girl was feeling a little tired. Still, she persevered and made that happen as well. It wasn't long before the wig finally came off, and one of her favorite beanies went on —a blueprint one, of course!

Food was still an issue, but she did her best.

All her siblings were there, and I was very thankful for many reasons. Most of all, I was grateful for the support not only for

Number 5 and the new life she was about to embark on but for Diane.

When it was time for the father-daughter dance, something else happened that I nor anyone else was expecting. It was when our oldest son walked over to his mom, Diane, and escorted her to the dance floor, and they danced together. Everyone was in tears, including the two of them!

It was awesome to see.

When the reception was winding down, it was time to get Diane back to the hotel for some much-deserved and needed rest. We got to our room, I got her ready for bed, and we settled in for the night. She and I talked a bit about the day's events and soon fell to sleep.

The next day we packed up, checked out, and came home. Up to this point in time, my whole focus and existence had become all about taking care of my best girl the best way that I could, and I was fine with that, totally full-on fine with that!

After the wedding, things started to progress at an even faster pace. Food intake had dropped considerably, potassium and blood pressure levels were still an issue, and the drain tubes were still in effect, and now the kidneys were acting up more.

Remember the previous chapter entitled 'A Sleeping Giant Has Awakened?' Well, I'm going to share with you why I wrote this title.

You see, when the fit began to hit the shan, after her 107-degree fever, I very strongly was under the belief that the fever had stirred up something inside her body, causing all of this mayhem.

I had mentioned it to a few of her doctors, and they didn't commit to confirming it one way or another, but they didn't totally dismiss the possibility either. From my heart to yours, please don't take fevers lightly, especially if they spike very high, very quickly.

I know many of you understand this already. Still, please address them appropriately because you never know what giant could be sleeping in your body or inside someone you love. Look at each other, and most importantly, listen to each other.

CHAPTER 14

Buddy The Wonder Dog!

"Sometimes we receive blessings that we either didn't know we needed or didn't even ask for...those are sometimes the best kind!"
(Bill Leone, 1962 - Present)

WE WERE NOW ABOUT to enter one of the most bizarre and scary times in our history. 2020 had just been born, and something terrible loomed in its doorway.

A new giant had been awakened in our world, and its name is...you guessed it... COVID 19 aka CORONAVIRUS!

Although it hadn't hit in full force just yet, the news channels and newspapers were beginning to talk about it and stress concerns to the public of its possible dangers that could come our way. Diane was becoming sicker and sicker every day, and now we had this to worry about!

In February, Diane started out the New Year by spending time in the hospital. It was another potassium issue, with a slight cold attached this time. During this stay it was discovered that she had a minor case of pneumonia in one of her lungs.

The doctors didn't seem to be too worried about it but still kept an eye on its progress. She was eventually released to come home in a few days as per SOP (Standard Operating Procedure).

Covid had been gaining ground but not enough to have kept me out of the hospital from being with my girl PTL! Once home, the mandates began to flood the airwaves in March/April, and non-essential workers were expected to stay home. I was considered an essential worker because I worked in various grocery stores helping to keep the shelves stocked as a merchandiser.

This meant I was still working and felt I needed to be for financial reasons. Most of my family was after me to stay home, and as hard of a decision as it was, I remained in the field for a bit longer.

Different government assistance programs were beginning to pop up, and I took advantage of one. My supervisor at the time was one of the best ones I have ever worked for, and she had no problem with me using the help at that time. She was aware of Diane's illness and was over-the-top supportive of me. I'll never forget her.

I stayed home for six weeks with my sweetheart, which was a significant relief for her siblings, and our kids while it created a much-needed break for them.

I knew I couldn't be out for very long, but it was, as we say, better than nothing, and Diane wasn't complaining about it too much anyway. Can't imagine why she would want to spend all day with me. Go figure (*wink wink*).

From here on, everybody was asked to wear a mask before entering our house.

Her doctor even said that I needed to wear a mask since I was still working in the field. Visitations were limited both in time and to the number of people present. I wasn't concerned with anyone's hurt feelings about the new home restrictions. Fortunately, those who knew the situation understood that I was only protecting Diane from this new kind of virus traveling through our air. It wasn't personal.

I knew if she caught this stuff, it would literally be the last time I would be with her because the hospitals had their new guidelines for visitation as well. She was always my number one priority, sick or not.

My time at home came to an end, and I went back out into the work field. Diane's needs were beginning to way heavily on her siblings as she became more dependent in relying on the physical strength of others. They were battling their own issues but still wanted to help with their sister's care. God bless them for the tremendous show of love.

I continued battling between wanting to stay home and to be with her or, to be the strong, responsible husband who would continue to bring the much-needed paycheck home.

One day, God reminded me of something: my place in this life was to be by her side for better or worse, in sickness and health, always. This wasn't a problem for me.

But I felt that at this particular point in time, God was telling me to be physically present with her and that it was okay to do so. And also, He would provide.

If you are of the way, then we all try to do our best to heed the call of the LORD. We had retirement savings to care for us and provide for our future as a retired couple.

I decided to use whatever was needed from that retirement fund to take care of us right then! So I stopped working and stayed home with her. It was one of the best decisions I had ever made.

When I spoke to Diane about this, she was all for it and seemed a bit relieved that I would be the one with her all the time. It wasn't anything against her siblings or our kids, for she really loved being with them also. She was embarrassed and seeing the strain that, in her mind, was putting everyone through stress weighed on her greatly. It made her feel bad even though we both knew that our family was there because they wanted to be and not because they had to be. It's just how she was in never wanting to be a burden —but she was never a burden.

Our oldest daughter and her daughter (our grandbaby) had come out to visit with us, and unbeknownst to me, she had decided to bring something special with her: PUPPIES!

Her two dogs, a dachshund, and a terrier had just had puppies. They were so cute, and each had already developed their little personalities. You could tell who the alpha and the runt were and everything in between.

Hindsight being 20/20, I think it was a setup from the beginning that our daughter and Diane had cooked up!

We had just lost our most recent pet, a golden retriever, a little while back, and I was not in the mood or ready to have another animal to take care of. Diane required a lot of attention, and I know what's needed to take care of a puppy. I didn't feel as though I had it in me to take care of both as it would distract me from Diane a little bit—my focus needed to be solely on her.

Well, Diane vetted out one particular little guy and began to make a connection with him. I saw the look in her eyes, and then she hit me with that face and that smile. How could I say no to her? She knew and understood my concerns beforehand, but once she saw him, it was all over! And of course, she named him: BUDDY!

What followed next was a whole menagerie of adventures and folly. Buddy, of course, proceeded to eat, chew, pee, and poo on everything everywhere he could. He was so small and fast that I had trouble catching him as he would run under things that weren't easy for me to get to, and it was quite the sight!

But the main thing was that it brought Diane some much-needed joy and distraction. And again, that smile was priceless. Honestly, I would have gotten her a whole litter if she wanted it.

We were then able to make it to just a few doctor appointments. While at one of them with her primary care doctor, he was really noticing her weight loss since he hadn't seen her for a bit. He presented the idea of having a feeding tube inserted.

For Diane, that was a very hard no. He would also ask her some tough questions about her long-term goals. They weren't easy to hear, and even harder to listen to her answers, knowing in your heart what she really wanted. Her wheelchair was being used more and more to help her move about, and then eventually, total reliance on it for mobility.

All of her issues up until that point had remained constant and consistent in their level of destruction.

Until recently, the newest development for Diane had been her looming kidney function problem. It had now become stage 4 renal failure. Fortunately, though dialysis was not on the table, she was beginning to experience slight lower back pain. Diane was dealing with it the only way she knew how: as if it wasn't there.

My girl had entered into a strange new stage of existence in her life. It was one of not wanting to die, yet she wasn't doing anything that would help her to live. It was like her mind was telling her what she should do, yet her heart was telling her what she wanted to do, and in turn, nothing would happen. We were all in a wait-and-see mode, including her.

Our Senior Pastor and friend knew about everything that was going on up until this point and had always offered for me to take whatever time that I needed to care for her. I was trying my best to remain faithful to the church, but finally, I took him up on his offer and stepped away from all of my church duties. I also took some time away from the police department.

It was hard for me to do, but as I stated before, my girl was my number 1 priority. We had been blessed to be surrounded by a lot of really good-hearted and genuine people, and all of them were behind us in whatever we may have needed during this time. I'm so thankful for them all.

I continued my battle with the company that supplied the drainage kits for her plural sacks since I didn't want to experience any type of outage while waiting for the new shipment to arrive. But it would happen anyway. After enough complaining, I was assigned a manager that I could place my order with directly, and it never happened again!

I guess it's really true that the squeaky wheel gets the grease!

Our family parties were always something to look forward to, and for a short time, Diane could still go to them, though it took a lot out of her. But COVID kind of halted that fun too. Instead, ZOOM became our newest family member, and we all made the best of it. It also made it easier for Diane to attend these events, though still not the same as in person.

By this time, Buddy had grown up pretty quickly, but he was still all puppy. I had nicknamed him "The Jaws Of Death" and "The Claws Of Terror." You all know how sharp puppy teeth are, and I have the scars and shredded clothes to prove it!

While he somewhat matured, he began to learn stuff on his own, and one of them was the fact that Diane, his mommy, was sick. When he would go near her, he would have a completely whole new attitude toward her. He moved slower towards her; his tail would gently wag, and he looked into her eyes as if to have a smile on his face.

It was one of the sweetest things I've ever seen an animal do. I was always a little worried as to how he would be around her. As Diane would be sitting on the couch, he would put his front paws up on her legs (while there was a very thick blanket to cover them for protection). In time, after proving himself by behaving, I would let him up by her, and he would just simply snuggle down beside her and stay there for quite a while. She really loved him.

But when he was around me, well, in his mind, I was there for only one purpose, and that was to be his human chew toy!

I was okay with it because to have him around made my girl smile, and that's all I cared about. He was one of those surprise blessings in more ways than one.

CHAPTER 15

Heartbreak Hotel Leone

Psalm 34:18 The Lord is close to the brokenhearted and saves those who are crushed in spirit.

NOW BEFORE DIANE getting sick, our oldest daughter had been having some marital issues off and on. During those times, she and her little girl often came out and stayed with us—we didn't mind. Things would seem to calm down, get worked out, and then back to Arizona, they would go. But there was something else much darker going on that we weren't fully aware of happening with her and how much of an issue it had become.

We knew that there was stuff that she needed to address and have had to for a very long time. There was still this outlying obstacle yet to be discovered to its fullest—alcoholism. As it got worse, it became harder for her to hide it. This was going on for quite some time and soon began to affect all of us, especially those closest to her.

She had been struggling with depression, back pain, and various other types of health and emotional issues for a very long time, which I believe led to her drinking problem. Things happened to her at a very young age that I won't be going into. Just understand that they were experiences that no one should have to go through at any age...ever!

I need to make something known about our daughter.

When she was sober, she was the most loving, caring, sweetest, best mom and person you would ever want to meet. She was fun, funny, and would be genuinely concerned about you and always there if you needed her.

She and Diane were really good together, and boy could she cook! She loved to use garlic and lots of it! She made the best ranch dressing/dip you ever had!

But when the drinking took over, it was like a switch got flipped, and the monster inside took over, and she became someone you didn't know even existed.

During one time of marital distress, she asked to come out and spend some time with us, and of course, as any loving parents would, we said yes. But this time, she didn't bring her daughter. It was just her, and she was in full alcoholic mode.

At the same time, Diane was in full sickness mode—not a good combination for me to deal with. Anyway, she showed up semi sober, but things soon took a turn for the worse.

The lying and the stealing began. We found bottles of alcohol hidden all over her room and in her car (YES! In her car!).

God was definitely watching over her because He kept her safe when driving and always got her home. We obviously confronted her, and it wasn't a good conversation. The bottom line was that I decided to send her home for the simple reason that I already had enough on my plate taking care of mom and wasn't able to always be watching over her as well. This may have sounded a bit cold, but this was tough love at its most challenging stage.

It was our daughter, and she needed help, yet I was sending her away. I was at my limits, and my girl was still priority Number 1. I felt terrible, to say the least. Our daughter went home and attended various programs to help her get better, yet none of them took hold.

I think that we were the last ones on her list of phone calls one evening after she had exhausted all of her other resources, namely our family. She was looking for money, and no one caved in and gave it to her.

Now, some of you know about the conversation that takes place next. It's the one where it turns into everyone else's fault as to why they are the way they are and not theirs.

Up to this point, we all had tried to love and support her the best we could from a distance because we were in two different states. But during this conversation, she said something that set me off. I lit into her and didn't back down. I couldn't handle hearing anymore about how our family was the blame for her issues. Diane was just sitting there listening to it all.

After I hung up the phone, I asked her if I had said and done the right thing. She was in total agreement with me. Normally, Diane would have been the lead in the conversation. We didn't hear from our daughter for a while until one day, we find out that she was missing and no one knew where she was.

She eventually ended up back where she lived and proceeded to drink more and take some pills. She was trying to commit suicide. I heard that she had called 911 on herself and then was taken to the hospital and placed in ICU.

Three of our kids went to be with her only to get there in time to watch their sister slip away from them. This was September of 2020, and once again, a new season had been established—we lost a child, and our kids lost a sister.

Remember, Diane was a super mom, to say the least, and this was destroying her inside. She was the type of mom that would have literally given her life for any of her children without question. She totally full-on loved all her kids. The day came for our daughter's memorial service, and I was starting to try and get Diane moving to be ready to go.

As I talked to her about it, she looked at me and said, "William, I can't go." I asked her if she was sure, and she reaffirmed that she couldn't do it. It was simply too much for her to handle.

So, I made a call to one of our friends that were going to be there and asked if they would come and be with Diane so that I could go.

This was a very dear friend of Diane's and of mine for many years, and she, of course said yes (This friend was the other third of LIGHT TOUCH). My girl's heart was broken into more pieces than I would care to count. The service was nice as we held it at our church. Though I couldn't do the service for obvious reasons, we had another pastor friend of ours do it for us.

COVID was still around, and I had to limit the number of people that wanted to attend. That wasn't easy, and I'm sure I ruffled a few feathers.

Diane had reached her weakest state, where even the wheelchair wasn't making a difference anymore.

More and more doctor appointments were having to be canceled and rescheduled until she just couldn't make them at all.

This presented a new problem, which was that she still needed to be seen and monitored by at least her primary care doctor.

Folks, we have been very blessed to have some really awesome people in the medical care industry put in her path. Her doctor was brainstorming, and the idea of palliative care was thrown into the mix. We weren't exactly sure of what was entailed in this type of care, but we found out quickly.

Even though palliative care would help with the traveling issues somewhat, meaning that someone would still come to your home to monitor your state of being, they didn't come often enough. Also, they were limited as to the type of care that they could give in the home.

Diane's needs bumped us into the next and final stage: hospice. This began in October 2020, about one month after our daughter's memorial.

Not many people like to hear that word because it usually only means one thing to the patient. It seemed like it was no time when they had moved in just about everything that Diane would need for this new phase.

Comfort and pain management was their goal, and the company that took care of my girl was excellent in that aspect.

A new adjustable hospital bed came, with a home oxygen unit that could run 24/7, along with many types of much-needed medical supplies. All I had to do was call, and it was usually there by the next day, if not sooner! But with all of this great care and service...it was still hospice.

Once everything had arrived, we positioned the items just right in the den that was at the back of our house. We set up an end table that would hold all the things that she wanted to be close to her reach, including her Bible. The usual stuff was there as well as Kleenex, chapstick, etc... Oh! And don't forget about the TV flippers! (Yes, I called them FLIPPERS!).

We had a great in-home nurse that would come two to three times a week as needed. She would even come if I needed her when she wasn't scheduled. They were even trying to take care of me somewhat. That was simply amazing. But the most important thing was for Diane to feel comfortable with her caregivers.

Of course, I was always there, keeping an eye on everything that went on while they were conducting their visit. The one thing that would throw off almost all medical staff is that they were never prepared for just how sensitive her skin was.

Almost always, and unintentionally, they would leave a mark on her. Our nurse quickly got familiar with that aspect because I trained her too!

Diane's world had become very small, while mine had exploded into something I never thought it could be. I now had many titles beginning with the obvious, which were husband, then caregiver, drainage tech, wound care specialist, cook/dietician, maid, pharmacist, and physical therapist!

If you never thought you were very good at multi-tasking, this new normal could change the way you feel very quickly.

When you're the only one there, you have no choice but to become *everything* they need you to be because you simply love them more than anything. Yes, it was a lot of work, but I'd do it again in a heartbeat because I knew she'd do it for me! It was a great honor and a privilege to take care of her, and it reminds me of a movie I saw many years ago called 'A Vow To Cherish.' It starred the actor from The White Shadow TV series, Ken Howard. Look it up if you get a chance. It was a real tear-jerker but worth seeing.

At that time, my caregiver chops were not at the level where they needed to be. So I had a crash course on certain techniques that would help in Diane's care. This training came from not only our wonderful hospice nurse but also from one of Diane's sisters, who had a very long and successful career as a head nurse and who would later retire after becoming Director of Nursing for an assisted living facility that spanned over many years. I must say, she knew her stuff!

One of my biggest challenges was being able to get Diane positioned and comfortable in her new bed. Fortunately for me, it was an easy fix and something that was easy to learn.

I soon became proficient at getting my girl all comfy cozy. Tada! Now, I have always loved Diane's meatloaf and was craving it for some reason. With my cooking talents being nonexistent, I decided to ask Diane to coach me on how to make *her* meatloaf recipe, and suddenly, there was that smile again!

She was in her bed, and I was in the kitchen—I might as well have been in the middle of the ocean!

Anyway, she would give me directions from her bed, and I would follow them to a "T." We used eggs, chopped onion, and some seasoning, mixed it all up, slapped it in a Pyrex, and through it in the oven! Voila! Meatloaf! It was the best meatloaf I ever had, and it wasn't because I made it. It was because she was able to make it through me. Yes, we did it together!

There aren't too many moments that you get with someone on hospice care that are fun and entertaining, but I tried my best to make every moment count, no matter what.

Many years before she had gotten sick, we would have this battle as to who loved each other more. She would always say, "I love you more," and I would come back at her with, "No, I love you more because I'm bigger, and you can't hold as much love inside you!" She would just give me a look as if to say, "You're such a goof!" That little routine stuck with us always, and we had that battle after the meatloaf was done cooking.

There was this moment in time where I became a little scared for my health and of what would happen to my girl if something happened to me. Well, I joined Weight Watchers and began a workout routine, and started to see results. I lost about 25 pounds, and my other health issues were improving, which made me happy to see that I was going to be able to be here for her and not laid up in some hospital.

I would go out in our garage for about 15 to 20 minutes almost everyday for a workout. The problem was that I needed to be able to hear Diane's call if she needed me.

My quick-thinking mastermind of a brain came up with this brilliant idea to call her on her phone and put both of them on speaker. That way, all she had to do was simply speak, and I would come running! It worked! There were many little and big obstacles that needed to be overcome, but we were able to do so for the most part.

If you are a caregiver, please remember how important it is for you to take care of yourself. The person you love is counting on you, and no matter how much of a burden they think they are for you, they need you to be okay.

One day, I received a call from Diane's primary care doctor.

He was calling to check on her as all doctor visits had stopped. During our conversation, I flat out asked him how much time do you think she had left. He very honestly responded without any hesitation and said it was between 3 to 4 months.

All I could say was wow, and he then advised me to spend as much time with her as possible.

Some of our friends were sensing that the time was drawing near and wanted to come by and see her too. I would always check with Diane first to see if she was up to it or not. If she was, I would keep the visits short and to a minimal amount of people at one time. If she wasn't up to it, I simply would pass that on to whoever was inquiring about a visit. Everyone was pretty understanding and didn't cause me any grief over it.

The only ones that I didn't put restrictions on were our kids and her siblings. One thing I did notice, though, was that when people were over visiting, Diane would seem to perk up just a little bit more and had a different glow about her. I'm not sure if she was putting up a good front or if visitors were helping her feel normal again, and maybe it was a little of both, I suspect. In the long run, it didn't really matter because it was good to see a little spark of life run through her tiny body.

If I hadn't mentioned it already, by this time, she had stopped taking all medications of her choice. I must admit, there were times when I showed my frustrations with all of that and would then regret it. Some of you may know how hard it is to watch someone just wither away and not be able to have any type of influence over them on that matter.

All you can seem to do is to honor their decision and carry on with the daily routine, whatever that entails.

CHAPTER 16

The Love Chapter

1 Corinthians 13:4-8 "4 Love is patient, love is kind. It does not envy, it does not boast, it is not proud. 5 It does not dishonor others, it is not self-seeking, it is not easily angered, it keeps no record of wrongs. 6 Love does not delight in evil but rejoices with the truth. 7 It always protects, always trusts, always hopes, always perseveres. 8 Love never fails..."

AFTER A HUSBAND AND WIFE are married, they will begin to enjoy certain physical intimacies that only a husband and wife should be privileged to enjoy. But because of Diane's illness, those special times had all ceased to exist. Although, they did seem to morph into something totally different and just as meaningful. Again, I'm not going to go into a lot of detail, but hopefully, I will be able to articulate what I'm trying to explain to you all.

You see, just because you can't touch someone the way that you used to doesn't mean that the love is gone or the relationship is over. To base your love for someone solely on a physical relationship would be a terrible mistake, to say the least. There is so much more involved than the sensuality of the relationship. Here's what I mean.

When my girl first got sick, the physical part of our relationship soon began to diminish and eventually disappeared. We would still hold hands and kiss and hug but those special times were gone. It was sad for both of us, but we still loved each other very deeply and made it known every day.

Something amazing started to happen with my heart. Through Diane's ever-increasing weakness, my love for her grew stronger and stronger. Stay with me here... As her body was not strong enough to fully take care of her everyday needs and hygiene issues, I became challenged with the task of filling in for her during those times of need.

Now, remember, I'm Blood & Guts, no problem, guy!...Poop & Puke: problem.

My sweetheart knew my boundaries and felt terrible that I had to go through these times with her and for her. But I have to share what was happening to me. I knew I needed to help her, and honestly, I wanted the job wholeheartedly!

But something needed to change inside me if I was going to be the man and the husband that she needed me to be. I began to pray like never before for the strength and the calmness needed to perform my duties as a caregiver for her. As usual, God was listening, and he showed up with a solution to help me help her. It worked, and I was able to take care of her in ways that I never thought that I could do.

It wasn't perfect, mind you, but I was able to be who she needed me to be. Again, stay with me here. The level of intimacy had shifted to a much deeper level than just one of sensuality. I was able to serve her beyond what we think of as normal and regular everyday activities in ways that no one else should have had to. I was actually falling more and more in love with her (as if that were even possible) all because of this change that took place and because she simply needed me. I couldn't let her down, nor wouldn't.

Folks, if you never thought you could love anyone more than you already do, think again! Just wait until something catastrophic happens, and then you take another look at yourself, then you take a look at your one and only. This may be a bad analogy, but you see this all the time in movies where the love interest gets shot or hit by a car or something terrible like that, and the other half comes running into the room just gushing with feelings for that person that they never knew they had, right?

I'm just trying to convey that being totally committed to someone means going all in—no matter what the cost.

If there are any of you going through or have gone through such a time, just know that my prayers are with you, from my heart to yours.

Reality was beginning to set in that this Christmas may be/was going to be her last Christmas.

We didn't want to admit it to ourselves or anyone else, for that matter. It was hard for me to even begin to think about what Christmas entailed for us this year because my total focus was on my best girl. With that in mind, I knew that my sweetheart absolutely loved Christmas. I dove in to make Christmas happen the best way that I could imagine.

Our youngest son and I decided one day to go out and find a tree. I really like the Nordmann trees. To me, they are kind of like a cross between a Douglas Fir and a Noble Fir: very full, and they last long! Anyway, we found a good one, loaded it in the truck, and home we went.

Diane was parked in the back room of the house, and we cleared a space for it right next to the TV so she could see it with no problems. I like gadgets and found this remote on/off flipper that would operate the tree lights. It was so cool, and Diane liked it too! That way, she could turn on the lights anytime she wanted.

Often at night, sometimes I would get up to go to the restroom, and I could see the Christmas glow of the tree lights coming from downstairs. She would turn them on when she couldn't sleep. I think they brought her a little comfort, and I was good with that. She also loved nativity scenes, and I think that I had one in almost every room of the house, including our front lawn!

Our son and I finished decorating the inside of the house, and then I ventured to the great outdoors to put up the outside lights. It wasn't the kind you saw in the movie Christmas Vacation, but they were still just as spectacular and didn't cause any blackouts! Upon completion, I would wait until nightfall and then take a picture to bring inside to show Diane. This always brought a smile to her face...you know the one.

Christmas shopping had a whole new look to it and not just because of Covid since we were housebound! Amazon became my new best friend for shopping, and shop we did! I would sit next to Diane's bed and talk over with her what she thought we should get and for who. We would then order together and wait for our shipments to come in. It went pretty smoothly for the most part. Although I still missed going out to the stores and actually seeing what we were buying beforehand...oh well.

Diane was especially hard to buy for because, by this time, she had so many limitations. Although, I was still able to find a few things for her.

As Christmas drew closer, I started planning an evening with our kids when we could all have our Christmas time together. We settled on a date to make it happen. It was a wonderful time, yet there were many mixed feelings and emotions.

On the one hand, we were celebrating Christmas. But on the other hand, we all knew what was looming in the near future. All in all, we still had an enjoyable evening. After our Christmas time with the kids was over, for the next few days leading up to the big event, Diane and I would enjoy our yearly holiday movies together. Her favorites were Little Women, White Christmas, and a couple of other ones. Mine was Christmas Vacation and Christmas Story.

I would light a fire, make us a couple of cocktails, and she'd turn on the tree lights as I would turn off all of the other ones. We'd have the most beautiful time together—just us, which was how I liked it. As Christmas Eve slowly came to an end, and when bedtime rolled around, I would stand next to her bedside, and she would lean her head into my hip. I'd bend down to kiss her goodnight and tell her I love her so much. This would then, of course, ignite our little battle of who loved who more, and another one of those smiles would be on her face...it was the best.

It was now Christmas Day. Just like I had done so many times before, I would begin my descent down the stairs into the room where my girl would be waiting for

me. Although, I must confess something to you. Every morning I made my way down those stairs, I prepared myself to see her gone.

Knowing that, I knew I'd feel cheated in some way by not getting to be with her because I knew that she didn't want to be alone when the time came. Fortunately, that never happened, but I still agonized over the thought.

She would already have the tree lights on and her favorite shows on the TV, which included any and all of the cooking shows!

For some reason, she really was drawn to those cooking shows. The how-to's, the contests, and all of the specialty-themed food shows. There were some other shows as well that she and I enjoyed watching together, like the hospital, fire, and police shows, just to name a few. For comedy shows, she absolutely loved Frazier, The Golden Girls, and Friends.

I must say, they had me laughing pretty hard at times, but mostly it was good to see her laughing like she used to do. When she got into a full-on roar, her whole body just shook, and she could hardly get a breath or speak. Not a sound came out of her!

Another Christmas had come and gone, and we made our way on towards the New Year. Normally, this would be the time of year when we would be making plans and reservations to go to our favorite beach house escape, but not this year.

Diane's body had gone into yet another new phase. All this time, she hadn't been eating or drinking much of anything, including not taking any meds. This, of course, kept her from receiving all of the much-needed good stuff to help her maintain life.

Bed sores had popped up and like they will do, gave Diane another source of pain, not to mention that the ointment that was supposed to keep the sores away stung when applied. There was no relief in sight for my poor girl. I know she had a high pain tolerance, but just how much can one person handle? We had stopped draining her chest because there was no more fluid build-up.

I'm still unsure if that was a good thing or just because of the lack of liquids in her body.

This new phase included something else that I wasn't ready to handle. I'm not gonna lie, but it was also a little bit scary!

It was so frightening I had to call the Hospice nurse to make a special nonscheduled visit, and like always, accommodated my request. She was out to see us early by the next day, along with one of Diane's sisters (who I also called), the one who is the retired director of Nursing.

This new phase was my most dreaded phase of all because it was confirming what the outcome was projected to be.

My sweetheart began hallucinating.

CHAPTER 17

Entering The Waiting Room

Psalm 23 "1 The Lord is my shepherd, I lack nothing. 2 He makes me lie down in green pastures, he leads me beside quiet waters, 3 he refreshes my soul. He guides me along the right paths for his name's sake. 4 Even though I walk through the darkest valley, I will fear no evil, for you are with me; your rod and your staff, they comfort me. 5 You prepare a table before me in the presence of my enemies. You anoint my head with oil; my cup overflows. 6 Surely your goodness and love will follow me all the days of my life, and I will dwell in the house of the Lord forever."

UPON HER ARRIVAL, I spoke to the hospice nurse in the front room of our house before entering the back section where Diane was staying. I wanted to have a little bit of privacy to explain to her what was happening. I didn't want to be saying any of this in front of Diane. I didn't want to frighten her anymore than she may already be feeling at this point.

I'm sure our nurse had seen this scenario many times before and was no stranger to the situation. It really takes a special person to be involved in providing this type of care when you know the outcome. I applaud caregivers in the hospice field.

She started her usual greeting and questions that she would have for Diane, along with the taking of her vitals.

We helped her get readjusted in her bed, changed her into clean bedclothes, put medicine on her bed sores, and finally got her all snuggled down and comfy as best we could.

When the nurse had completed her time with us that day, she filled in the hospice notebook that they provided for us with all the

149

information that I would need in case I had any questions or if there were any problems that might arise. I signed off that she was there just like every other time, and then I walked her to the front door and had one more conversation with her.

She did her best to explain to me what was happening and then what was going to happen next. It was hard to take in what she was saying because it wasn't registering with me right away.

I felt like I was watching someone else's life being played out and not ours, but it soon sank in. The hospice nurse began to inform me that now was the time to start Diane's comfort meds (lorazepam and morphine).

I was given the new medicine schedule to begin immediately. Of course, I asked an obvious question which was, "How much longer?" She confidently, yet gently replied, "Maybe three to four days".

I then thanked her for being so good to my girl, and then she left. I went back to where Diane and her sister were and I heard her ask her sister something about the hallucinations. She asked her if this was bad (meaning the hallucinations).

Her sister nurse had to think fast and replied with something like, "Well, I think you need more oxygen because that can cause you to see things." It was almost like we were trying to convince ourselves that what was happening really wasn't happening. It may have worked but for a moment.

Diane had become restless and agitated, but sister nurse told her that I would start giving her the refrigerator medicine that would help make her feel better. That information alone seemed to calm her down a bit.

Suddenly, it was Friday evening, and New Year's Eve had arrived. Everyone had gone home, and it was back to just me and my sweetie. As we settled in and watched our New Year's Eve shows, the hallucinations were even more present than before.

One of the things she sensed was that there were people behind her trying to play pranks on her. I would be right there to assure her that no one was here but us. At one point, she even thought that I was in on it!

I finally gave in to trying to convince her that no one was in the room with us and simply told her that I would tell them to stop—that seemed to work for a while. We kissed each other while ushering in the New Year, and I told her I loved her so much.

I then gave her another round of the new meds, as instructed by the hospice nurse, and we said our good nights.

As I turned to make my way up the stairs, she quietly asked me if I would spend the night downstairs with her. It wasn't something that I hadn't done before, and I was totally willing to do this for her...especially knowing that we were short on time.

So I grabbed a blanket and my pillow and snuggled in on the couch, which had a reclining chair built into it. It wasn't the best night's sleep I've ever had, but it didn't matter because my girl needed me and I wasn't going to let her down.

It was now Saturday, New Year's Day, and one of our anniversaries no less. I had decided that today was the day that the family should have some time with her and say their goodbyes while she was still semi-coherent. It was open to immediate family only, which included her siblings (and spouses), and our kids (and spouses).

When they all showed up, I backed away and let everyone take their time and didn't rush the day.

As you can imagine, there were many tears, gentle caresses, kisses, hugs, and love that filled the entire room. Everything was going along as smoothly as it could have under the circumstances. But just when you thought things couldn't get more complicated, one of our daughters had been exposed to someone that had Covid-19.

I had to tell our daughter, that was exposed, that she couldn't come until everyone else had left because we didn't want to expose anyone in the family to the virus. I felt terrible but had to do it. After some time had passed, everyone left and went home.

I then called my daughter to come over. When she got there, I waited outside while she had her time with her mom. When she was through, she made her way to the backyard where I was and just broke down in tears.

She was so hurt that she couldn't be there with all of us. I told her that this was more than what a hospital would have been able to offer because, at the time, no one was allowed in to see anybody, no matter what the reason was! I know she understood, but it still sucked—it was her mom.

Sunday morning had rolled around and I had plans to make the arrangements needed at our family mortuary.

Our oldest son and I went over to take care of things.

I must have been in one of my compartmental modes because I don't know how else I was able to think clearly enough to take care of business. Looking back now, it was God in control, as always.

We ended up in a really nice spot that was close to other family that was there. I remember so many times Diane would say, "I wish my mommy was here," in times of need. Well, as God would provide, we found a spot right next to her folks and jumped on it!

Our son and I finished taking care of business at the cemetery and returned home were Number 5 and Diane's sister nurse were hanging out with Diane. I had never told my girl where I was going.

In my mind, I was actually thinking that we had at least a few more days beyond the weekend—I was soon corrected.

Her regiment of comfort meds continued, and she slowly began to relax more and more, drifting off into dreamland. Our oldest son, Number 5, and sister nurse all hung out for a little while longer until they finally decided to go home and give me some time with her.

Sister nurse had this really special and comforting way of stating the fact that someone is knock, knock, knockin' on heaven's door. She would say, "They're entering the waiting room," and my best girl was there right now.

All the I's had been dotted, and the T's have been crossed.

Her salvation was intact, and she, like her mommy, was ready.

I just wasn't all that sure that I was ready just yet and not so soon. My brain was telling me that it was a good thing because she wouldn't be suffering anymore, but my heart was painfully breaking, and my body had a numbness come rushing over it.

In those next twenty minutes, all I could do now was to sit next to her at her bedside as I had done so many times before, hold her hand, and tell her that I love her so much.

Soon, her breathing began to get slower and slower.

They say that people in this state can still hear you but just can't respond, so I began to talk to her. I remember telling her that it was okay for her to go and that I'll be alright...but I was totally lying!

After I gave her permission to go, her grip tightened on my hand, and jerked a little bit. It really caught me off guard, and I began to get a little excited that maybe, I was going to get just a little more time with her. But more than likely, it was that she really did hear me and was saying, "All right then, I can go now."

The length of time between her breaths was now longer until finally, she stopped breathing altogether.

At about 4:43 PM on January 3, 2021, and barely three months after we had lost a daughter, my girl ran off with another man— but I was okay with it...his name is Jesus. She may have lost the battle, but she won the war! PTL!

As expected, I needed some time to gain some sort of composure before I could call everyone back to the house. Everyone came back that was there from that day and from the day before.

Fortunately, I had just made arrangements with the mortuary that morning, so when I called them to come, there were no issues. Also, I had to call the hospice company to make everything official. By this time, the numbness had fully taken over me, and like so many times before, compartmentalization was making it possible for me to be able to take care of business.

But trust me when I say that after the smoke had cleared, I was nothing short of a puddle of tears and unable to do or able to think much about anything other than this moment in time, one that I'll never forget but sometimes wish I could if only for a little while.

With Covid-19 still lurking in the wings, we were able to have her memorial service at the graveside as opposed to being inside with limited occupancy. This allowed for as many people to come as they wanted to. It was a good turnout, but that was no surprise to me.

She was an amazing person and had touched many lives throughout her time here, and the attendance spoke loud and clear to that effect.

Our Senior Pastor and friend conducted the service as our kids and a couple of other family members were the pallbearers. It was a beautiful day and a beautiful service. She was honored well.

As our friend had closed out our time with words of encouragement and prayer, folks offered their condolences and began to leave, but I couldn't just yet. Together, she and I could conquer anything. But the one thing we couldn't overcome together was AL Amyloidosis.

In addition, our MO, when dealing with tough situations, was to see it through to the end, and that's exactly what I was going to do today, by staying till the last shovel of dirt was placed over the top of my girl.

Now, as believers, we know that our loved ones are not there anymore and that what's in the ground is nothing more than an empty shell. The Bible refers to it as an old tent that we have moved out of to have traded up for a brand new tent in heaven, one that is perfect in form and in health. No more pain, suffering, weeping, no more physical afflictions, or deformities; we are made whole again in body and in spirit. Nonetheless, I still needed to be there till the end...for the last finishing touches...for me.

A reception was to follow, and again, we kept it to immediate family only because of Covid. All in all, I would call it a good day, and everyone that was there was supposed to be there. We enjoyed each other's company and loved on each other the rest of the day until, once again, it was time for all to go home.

It was a very strange feeling to be in this big house all by myself. But let's not forget about Buddy The Wonder Dog!

It wasn't until later that I began feeling that Diane wanted the dog for more than just herself. I feel that she knew what was coming and wanted Buddy for me so I wouldn't be alone and to have some sort of company.

I must say, though, that as much as he is a pain in you know what, sometimes I'm really glad he's here. My sweetheart was always looking out for me, even when she was sick. Other than the occasional Buddy eruption that day, the house was totally void of any sound.

Being a musician, you tend to hear any and all various sounds and nuances of the surroundings that you're in. This house, my house, was completely silent and still. It was like it knew that something was missing, and for the time being, it decided to mourn the loss. Or maybe, it was just all me.

CHAPTER 18

Unspoken Goodbyes

"How lucky I am to have something that makes saying goodbye so hard."
— A.A. Milne (Winnie-the-Pooh)

AS MY FAMILY WAS surrounding Diane that day, knowing that Jesus was on His way to take her home and saying their last goodbyes, one of the many things that were racing through my head at that particular moment was the fact that she and I never got to have our last goodbyes. But there was a reason why our last goodbyes never happened.

Anytime that Diane and I would be talking about 'whatever' stuff, the conversation would start to move towards those words that are hard to say but needed and or wanted to be said and made known to each other.

For most of us who've been in the same situation, it was usually the last time that you would ever get to say such heartfelt things to each other before the person you loved would begin to slip away, and the chance would be gone forever.

For Diane, in her mind, it signified that all hope was lost and made her feel as if she/we had given up. Besides the obvious, which is that she may not have been able to get anything out because of her breathing issues anyway.

Just the thought of what she would want to say brought her to tears and would only complicate and most likely frustrate her. When we would get to that point of sharing those feelings, she would very sweetly just hold up her pointer finger and gently wave it in the air as if to say, "Nope! We're not going to talk about this now!"

I understood and honored her wishes, but I somehow felt a little bit cheated. Then again, the reality of it was that I already knew how much she loved me and what I meant to her, and she already knew the same from me.

That being said, we had our unspoken goodbyes.

Now, I'm not really a greedy person, but when it came to her, I was. Greedy, meaning that I always wanted to spend more time with her no matter what it was that we were doing.

Greedy, meaning that I wanted her to see her two newest grandbabies: both boys! Greedy, meaning that I wanted to go on more adventures with her and to be able to truly grow old with her. Greedy, meaning that I wanted her back because she was taken from me too soon, and I wasn't ready yet!

I needed to hear one more "I Love You," share one last hug and kiss, spend just a few moments more in prayer together, and be able to have one last gaze into each other's eyes, the one that lets them know that they are your one and only for always.

Is it strange for someone to feel as if closure hasn't been fully achieved unless you get to share those last goodbyes?

Maybe it's just me again wanting to do this.

Or maybe, I just want her to hear from my heart one last time about how much she has meant to me and how much I've cherished having her in my life.

I never was much of a card giver, but today I think I might be able to rattle off a few lines for my girl. Here goes.

Hi DerDer.

I have some things I need to tell you.

In all of the relationships that I have had, all of the love combined, never even came close to the love I have for you.

158

You unselfishly and unconditionally gave me so much of you no matter what was

going on in your life or how you were feeling at the time. It was the best feeling in the world just knowing that I had you by my side in all things.

If somehow I knew of what was to be in our future, I would have still married you. The ride with you was worth the fall ("Didn't We Almost Have It All" - Whitney Houston).

You and I lived a lot of life in what seemed to be a short amount of time, but I was ready for more.

You were my wife, my love, and my best friend. I trusted you above all others, fully and completely. You knew everything about my life and all of my deep dark secrets that no one else knew. My heart was safe with you. I never cheated on you, nor did I ever want to. I only ever wanted to be with you, sweetheart.

You gave me a family to love and a life that was full.

You were the best part of me. If I could have, I would've gladly traded places with you.

You are totally full-on a better mom than I am a dad...and totally a better Nana than I am a Papa.

I'll miss our quiet times together as well as our hectic ones.

I'll miss you not being at our family gatherings.

I'll miss shopping, riding bikes with you, and watching our special movies that we liked over and over again. I'm going to miss how clingy you were at night and having you fall asleep in my lap just before bedtime.

I'm going to miss looking at my sweet-faced girl to see you looking back at me with nothing but love in your eyes.

I'll miss our silly times and especially all of the goofy names that we had for each other that came from movies. I will miss those sometimes silly sayings that you had for almost any occasion. The one I will remember most is the one you said every night after I would tell you that I'd see you in the morning. You always came back with, LORD willing!

Our Ireland trip remains in my heart and on my mind as if it were yesterday! You were awesome to be with!

The time of 10:10 PM will forever have an alarm set to go off, always reminding me of the time when I asked you to marry me in our park, and it will play one of our favorite songs: "Get Here."

Diane, you have made such an impact on my life and will continue to do so. I am so proud to have been your husband and even more honored that you let me. I know we aren't perfect people, but you were perfect for me.

Now DerDer, please don't try and tell me to move on with my life and that it's okay to find someone else. Unless God literally beats me over the head with a sign to do such a thing, I'm very content with going out on top, 'cause sweetie, you're going to be a tough act to follow!

I'm not going to put you away in my memories to only pull you out at certain times of the year.

I want you with me always. I don't want to be over you! I know Jesus is coming for you soon, and I'm happy that it's Him. I just wish we had more time.

My life with you has meant everything to me, and I will never forget about all of the adventures that we shared together: the good, the bad, and the ugly.

I'm gonna miss everything about you.

You will forever be My Girl, and I will forever be your... Mr. William.

Well, I did it. Do I feel any better? Not sure just yet, but I don't think it hurt.

At this point, it's been about a year and a half since Diane had graduated to be with the LORD, but it still feels like it was only a day or so ago.

I think, depending on what your relationship was with the one who passed, it plays a part in how you mourn for them.

Diane's siblings lost a sister. Her children lost a mother. I lost a wife. And not to mention, in the midst of it all, there was the loss of one of our daughters, which threw in a whole other dynamic to our mourning process.

During this time, I experienced many new emotions to include what I was calling "Firsts." These are the things that you experience for the first time without your mate. Some things were big, and some small, and some of them I wasn't even thinking about until they happened.

For example, the first time that I got sick, there was no one there to help take care of me. I was on my own. Anyway, you get the picture.

I ran across another one of Diane's journal entries dated December 12, 2017, and it was in regard to her first finding out about what kind of condition her heart was in and that it wasn't working properly to pump the blood the way it needed to be.

She mentioned that she was sad, discouraged, and scared.

But in the next paragraph, you begin to see the kind of woman of faith she really was.

In her own words, Diane wrote, *"This morning I am still scared, but more hopeful and know what I need to do. I need to LIVE each moment of every day and trust God. This simple verse that He gave me this morning brought much hope and was a reminder to draw closer to Him now more than ever before."* The verse that God gave her was 2 Corinthians 5:7 *"For we walk by faith, not by sight."*

The Word of God tells us in Hebrews 12:2 (Diane's favorite verse, BTW), *"Let us fix our eyes on Jesus, the author, and perfecter of our faith, who for the joy set before him endured the cross, scorning its shame, and sat down at the right hand of the throne."*

There was nothing wrong with her heart (if you know what I mean).

Folks, there is hope to be had in all things, and miracles can still happen in all things. But you ask yourself, "Why did Diane still have to die so soon and not get healed from this disease? Where was *her* miracle?"

Well, maybe it wasn't the type of healing or miracle in the way we all wanted it to be, but she did get healed, and she did receive her miracle when the LORD took her home.

Amen and Amen!

My life with my wife was nothing short of amazing, and I'll always hold on to her memory tightly in my mind and deep within my heart. I wanted it to go on forever.

Instead, God has given me a new adventure to experience and one that I hope will be just as amazing but different.

I saw this engraving while visiting a popular cemetery one day and thought it would be something comforting to think about at those special times in our lives. I would like to share it with you.

"We've known so much of happiness, we've had our cup of joy, and memory is one gift of God that death cannot destroy." (author unknown)

I pray that you all will get to have such an adventure in your lifetime. One that fills your days richly and completely and without regret. But most of all, to be filled with the greatest of these...LOVE.

"If nothing ever changed, we wouldn't have memories."
(Bill Leone, 1962 - Present)

Peace be with you,
Mr. William

About the Author

REV. BILL LEONE is an ordained Elder in the Church of the Nazarene and is the Associate Pastor/Worship Pastor at Faith Church of the Nazarene in Burbank, Ca. He also volunteers as a Police Chaplain in the same city.

Bill has been blessed with a gift from God (beginning at the age of 4), allowing him to become an accomplished musician who longs to share it with others.

He has lead worship at various adult and children's events and has written children's praise and worship songs for many VBS events. In addition, Bill has traveled throughout the U.S. entertaining and giving concerts on the organ, piano, and keyboards as a product specialist for various instrument manufacturers.

He got married in 1993, and is a dedicated, and loving father of a very blended family with 5 children, and 5 grand babies (for now!).

With Bill, what you see is what you get...always maintaining a high integrity, is a priority for Him.

I hope you enjoy getting to know Bill's heart for the LORD, and for others.

Resources

Alcoholics Anonymous www.aa.org

Suicide Prevention Resource Center www.sprc.org

National Suicide and Crisis Lifeline Dial 988 or Text 988

National Suicide Prevention Hotline 1-800-273-8255

Crisis Text Line Text Hello to 741741

Youth Line Text teen2teen to 839863, or call 1-877-968-8491

SAMHSA National Helpline 1-800-662-4357 (Substance Abuse and Mental Health Services Administration)

The Amyloidosis Foundation www.amyloidosis.org Donations can also be made.

Author Bill Leone contact info: Email: audible_angel@hotmail.com Website: www.audibleangel.com Book website: www.mylifewithmywife.org

Publisher & PR Contact Info: Diane@RebelBooksPress.com

CPSIA information can be obtained
at www.ICGtesting.com
Printed in the USA
BVHW051127041122
651156BV00007B/287

9 798986 893129